THE GOOD, THE BAD, AND THE UGLY
PITTSBURGH PIRATES

HEART-POUNDING, JAW-DROPPING, AND GUT-WRENCHING MOMENTS FROM PITTSBURGH PIRATES HISTORY

John McCollister

TRIUMPH
BOOKS

Library of Congress Cataloging-in-Publication Data

McCollister, John.
   The good, the bad, and the ugly Pittsburgh Pirates : heart-pounding, jaw-dropping, and gut-wrenching moments from Pittsburgh Pirates history / by John McCollister.
      p. cm.
   Includes bibliographical references.
   ISBN-13: 978-1-57243-982-5
   ISBN-10: 1-57243-982-3
   1. Pittsburgh Pirates (Baseball team—History. I. Title. II. Title: Pittsburgh Pirates. III. Title: Heart-pounding, jaw-dropping, and gut-wrenching moments from Pittsburgh Pirates history.

GV875.P5M394 2008
796.357'640974886—dc22

                                                        2007040524

This book is available in quantity at special discounts for your group or organization. For further information, contact:

Triumph Books
542 South Dearborn Street
Suite 750
Chicago, Illinois 60605
(312) 939-3330
Fax (312) 663-3557

Printed in U.S.A.
ISBN: 978-1-57243-982-5
Design by Patricia Frey
All photos courtesy of the Pittsburgh Pirates, except where otherwise indicated.

To Sally O'Leary. She has served the Pittsburgh Pirates and its Alumni Association since 1964. All Pirates fans owe her a standing ovation.

CONTENTS

FOREWORD

I've got to be among the proudest men in the world.

I have a wonderful wife, Karen, who is living proof that I am an overachiever. I have fathered two sons who would be the envy of any parent since Adam and Eve, I get to spoil five grandchildren, and I've been blessed with a rewarding, 10-year career in Major League Baseball with a team that's rich in tradition and remains filled with hopes for the future.

As a player and, later, as a broadcaster and a vice president for the Pittsburgh Pirates, I have been privileged to gain a unique perspective of the game. As a result, I can tell you with all certainty that the Pirates franchise, for more than a century, has offered Pittsburghers exciting baseball by players who do everything they can to win.

Consider the outstanding players who have donned the black and gold of the Buccos: Honus Wagner, Arky Vaughan, Pie Traynor, the Waner brothers, Vernon Law, Bob Friend, Ralph Kiner, ElRoy Face, Dave Parker, Bill Mazeroski, Willie Stargell, Andy Van Slyke, Jack Wilson, and Jason Bay. Oh, yes, there was also that right fielder with an unorthodox approach to the game—Roberto something or other.

As you read this book, I hope you see that the "good" of the Pirates far outweighs the "bad" or the "ugly." I hope, too, that it strengthens your loyalty to the Bucs—one of the premier teams in Major League Baseball.

One final note: when I was growing up in Connecticut, I could never have imagined that I would join the list of those players who remain so much a part of Pittsburgh's history. If there is a key to any success I may have enjoyed in baseball, it's that veterans of the game were willing to invest their time and counsel in someone who wanted very much to be a big-league ballplayer. To all of them, I owe my heartfelt thanks.

That reason is one of many why I decided to devote so much of my energy to the support of the Pittsburgh Pirates Alumni Association. This organization has dedicated itself to providing opportunities for inner-city kids to play the greatest game ever invented. You might call it my way of "giving back." If so, I am not shy about admitting that, through the work of the association, perhaps—just perhaps—some youngster who would otherwise be headed for a life of poverty with little hope for a successful future can grasp the opportunity to turn his life around.

If this happens because of something I've been able to do in cooperation with the Alumni Association, it would be one more reason for this guy to be proud. Mighty proud, indeed.

—Steve Blass

ACKNOWLEDGMENTS

No book is ever written in a vacuum. Helping with a project such as this is a crew of friends of the Pittsburgh Pirates, without whose help this volume would have been impossible.

Special thanks goes to Pittsburgh marketing and public relations consultant Todd Miller for assisting with editing and fact checking. Also, kudos to Robert Snodgrass and Laine Morreau of Triumph Books for their guidance.

To the family of the Pittsburgh Pirates, especially to Jim Trdinich and Dan Hart for their help in gathering photos, and to Steve Blass, Joe Billetdeaux, and Sally O'Leary of the Pirates Alumni Association for their support of charities dear to the heart of Pittsburghers everywhere, we give a rousing thanks.

And thanks to the Pirates Alumni Association as a whole. Founded in 1986, the Alumni Association raises and disburses funds for local charities, promotes baseball at the amateur and professional levels through past and present player involvement, and provides aid to former Pirates and their families through its Special Assistance Program. For more information or to make a tax-deductible donation, call 412-325-4788.

Finally, here's a salute to you fans of Pittsburgh who, for more than a century, have supported our Bucs through thick and thin. The marriage between you and the Pirates is one that will last as long as the Steel City exists. You're the greatest.

THE GOOD

Throughout the story of the Pittsburgh Pirates, a legion of magical moments and legendary players has emerged not only to make headlines, but also to bestow upon their fans certain unforgettable memories.

We shall forever cherish these treasures that include the most dramatic World Series in the history of baseball and a flashy right fielder who set the standard for excellence.

While we could fill an entire volume with just the "good" shown by the Buccos, here are a few instances that will hopefully bring back a pleasant memory or two.

THE 1960 PIRATES: THE SEASON, THE GAME, THE HIT

The year 1960 marked the beginning of remarkable changes in American history. A young Roman Catholic senator named John Fitzgerald Kennedy was elected president of the United States, and the so-called establishment suddenly realized that the torch of leadership had passed to a new generation. It was the start of the "Age of Aquarius" that challenged heretofore accepted norms about the family, for blind obedience to the letter of the law, even for faithfulness to the religion in which a person was raised.

Prior to 1960, Major League Baseball also embraced its own set of traditional standards. The reserve clause bound players inextricably to their teams unless they were traded or released. Players

1

signed autographs whenever possible—without charging. When a manager gave an order, he was obeyed without question. And, of course, the New York Yankees were expected to win the World Series.

Pirates fans recall with fond remembrance how their beloved Bucs shattered that last prediction.

From the minute the Pittsburgh ballclub set foot on the diamond on April 12 in Milwaukee, an aura of hope engulfed its players, manager, coaches, and fans. The Pirates lost the season opener, but just five days later, during an Easter Sunday double-header, they transformed dreams into genuine expectations. Pitcher Bob Friend blanked the Cincinnati Reds on a masterfully pitched game in the first contest. Game 2 offered a preview of coming attractions when Pittsburgh, down 5–0 going into the ninth inning, "rose from the dead." Hal Smith's three-run homer and Bob Skinner's game-winning shot into the right-field stands produced a come-from-behind 6–5 victory.

What made the Bucs a miracle team that year? Part of the reason was the solid core of players that filled its roster. Along with Skinner and backup catcher Smith, general manager Joe L. Brown molded a team with a formidable lineup that included catcher Forrest "Smoky" Burgess, hard-hitting first baseman Dick Stuart, center fielder Bill Virdon, third baseman Don Hoak, short-stop Dick Groat (that year's National League batting champion and winner of the Baseball Writers Association of America's Most Valuable Player Award), second sacker Bill Mazeroski, and an exciting right fielder with a heap of promise named Roberto Clemente.

Complementing these everyday players was a mound staff of aces that included 20-game-winner Vernon Law, Bob Friend (UPI's Comeback Player of the Year), Harvey Haddix, and relief specialist ElRoy Face. General Manager Brown initiated a favorable midsea-son trade by swapping the talented infield prospect Julian Javier to the Cardinals for veteran southpaw Wilmer "Vinegar Bend" Mizell.

Another important part of the picture of success was a tobacco-chewing, cigar-smoking craggy Irishman who wore No.

Waving his arm in the air, Bill Mazeroski crosses home plate on that memorable October 13, 1960, and becomes immortal in the hearts and minds of Pirates fans everywhere.

40 and sat in the far corner of the dugout. Manager Danny Murtaugh, now in his fourth year as Pirates skipper, employed not only a keen sense of baseball awareness and pragmatic leadership, but also a delicious sense of humor that went a long way to ease tensions normally associated with running a big-league team. This product of Chester, Pennsylvania, responded to one caustic critic, "I'd like to have that fellow who hits a home run every time, who strikes out every batter when he's pitching, and who never makes a mistake on the field. The only trouble is getting him to put down his beer and come down out of the stands."

A DEVASTATING BLOW

The late commissioner of Major League Baseball, Dr. A. Bartlett Giamatti, once wrote: "Baseball is meant to break your heart." Seldom do defeats of a team affect fans as much as do losses on a baseball diamond.

Bill Mazeroski's Series-winning home run on October 13, 1960, was no exception.

Barry Altman, a rabbi in Ormond Beach, Florida, still recalls that moment when he was in middle school growing up in the Bronx. "I was so overcome with emotion," he remembers, "that I actually hid underneath our front porch so I wouldn't have to go to school and face my classmates."

Sportscaster Bob Costas, who carries Mickey Mantle's baseball card in his wallet, said, "As an eight-year-old Yankees fan in 1960, I literally wept when Bill Mazeroski's home run cleared the ivy-covered wall at Forbes Field. Today, I have come to terms with it and can see Mazeroski for what he really was—one of baseball's all-time great players."

Finally the 1960 Pirates were blessed with two intangibles. The first was a simple but catchy slogan: "Beat 'em Bucs." It appeared on bumper stickers of family cars and on windows of offices at Westinghouse. It was pasted on school notebooks of teenagers who proudly displayed the black and gold catchphrase praising their hometown heroes.

The other rallying cry for the team was a pep song sung to the tune of "Camptown Races," with an equally simplistic treatment as the slogan. It had a chorus: "The Bucs are going all the way...all the way this year."

Neither of these gems would go down in the history of poetic immortality, yet they were enough to spark the enthusiasm of players and fans alike as the Pirates seesawed in and out of first place until July 27. On that day, they "came of age" and settled into the league lead to stay.

Pirates fans responded with unbridled enthusiasm, marching through turnstiles as never before. On September 12, the club set a new single-season attendance record by passing the old mark of

1,517,021 set back in 1948. Champagne corks popped 13 days later when Chicago mathematically eliminated the second-place St. Louis Cardinals from the pennant race and, for the first time in 33 years, the Pirates were kings of the National League.

By season's end, grabbing headlines for the pennant-winning Bucs were pitchers Law (20–9), Friend (18–12), Mizell (13–5), Haddix (11–10), and Face (10–8). Swinging the big clubs were Groat (.325, two home runs), Clemente (.314, 16 home runs), Smith (.295, 11 home runs), Burgess (.294, seven home runs), Hoak (.282, 16 home runs), Skinner (.273, 15 home runs), Mazeroski (.273, 11 home runs), and Stuart (.260, 23 home runs).

Seeing the "National League Champions" flag fly over Forbes Field was one big thrill. Raising one that announced Pittsburgh as the winner of the World Series would be even greater.

Only one thing stood in the way: the mighty New York Yankees.

The last time the Pirates had appeared in a World Series was in 1927, when they faced the likes of Babe Ruth, Lou Gehrig, and the "Murderers' Row" Yankees. This year seemed to be no different. The new Yankees flexed another set of muscles known as Mickey Mantle (40 HR), American League MVP Roger Maris (39 HR and a league-leading 112 RBIs), Yogi Berra, William "Moose" Skowron, Bobby Richardson, Tony Kubek, and Elston Howard, along with pitchers Edward "Whitey" Ford, Art Ditmar, and "Bullet" Bob Turley.

Guiding the 1960 edition of the Yankees (deemed by some experts as the second-best assembly of Bronx Bombers ever) was the crafty Charles Dillon "Casey" Stengel, now in his 10th World Series with the Yankees, who had led his team to seven world championships.

The "unbeatable" Yankees were odds-on favorites to take the Series in four or, at most, five games. Some local bookies in New York refused to take any bets, because so few customers would risk money on the Pirates.

Pittsburgh fans would not lose enthusiasm for their team simply because of predictions by some shady gamblers. Even the Federal Court downtown took a semiholiday when a judge announced court would be in session from 9:30 AM until 11:30 AM on game days.

The heads of baseball gurus shook in amazement when Pittsburgh squeaked out a 6–4 victory in Game 1 at Forbes Field. Law's admirable pitching and Mazeroski's home run overcame clouts out of the park by Maris and Howard.

As if to say, "Enough is enough," the Yankees rolled up their sleeves and pummeled the Pirates in Games 2 and 3 by scores of 16–3 and 10–0.

Law and Face limited the Yankees bats to eight hits in a 3–2 victory in Game 4 that was highlighted by a game-saving, leaping catch by Virdon in center field that robbed slugger Bob Cerv of a sure double.

Roger Maris clubbed a home run in Game 5, but that didn't offset timely doubles by Burgess, Groat, Mazeroski, and Virdon, as Haddix and Face allowed only five hits in a 5–2 win.

Instrumental in the Pirates' World Series victory over the New York Yankees in 1960 were (left to right) pitchers Vernon Law and ElRoy Face, and out-fielder Bill Virdon.

Back in Pittsburgh for Game 6, even the most pessimistic fan joined in the chorus of the theme song, "The Bucs Are Going All the Way." Whitey Ford muzzled the singing when he white-washed the Pirates for the second time in the Series, 12–0. Pittsburgh bats were tame, with only seven singles all afternoon.

All of this was but an overture to *the* game and *the* hit—both of which faithful Pirates fans continue to speak of with awe and reverence.

The early-morning sun peeking over the horizon on October 13, 1960, brought out a colorful fall kaleidoscope of scarlet, lemon, and gold leaves still clinging to the trees in Schenley Park, just beyond the outfield walls of Forbes Field. It seemed as though some of nature's finery wanted to linger just to witness what was about to happen.

Were any fiction writer to have submitted to a publisher the script for the 1960 World Series, especially for Game 7, it probably would have been rejected as being "unrealistic." But that's just one of the rewards of baseball; the predictable is not an ironclad guarantee.

Manager Murtaugh, in a gutsy move, benched his leading home-run hitter, first baseman Stuart, in favor of the better fielding Rocky Nelson. Law started on the mound for Pittsburgh, while Turley was the choice of Yankees manager Stengel.

Law set the Yankees down in order in the first. With two outs, Skinner walked in the Pirates' half of the inning. Nelson then made Murtaugh look like a genius when he parked a 2–1 pitch into the right-field stands for a home run, giving the Bucs a 2–0 lead.

The packed house of 36,683 continued to cheer in the second inning as Stengel removed starting pitcher Turley in favor of rookie Bill Stafford following a single by Smoky Burgess. A walk, a bunt single, and a single by Virdon doubled Pittsburgh's total to a more comfortable 4–0 lead.

Moose Skowron's homer in the fifth gave the Yankees their first tally. Following a single and a walk in the Yankees' half of the sixth, Murtaugh replaced Law with forkball specialist ElRoy Face. A single by Mantle made the score 4–2, and a long home run by Yogi Berra gave New York a 5–4 lead.

THE TEAM OF THE 20TH CENTURY

Baseball fans of any team in Major League Baseball engage in often heated debates on who were the greatest players throughout the team's history at various positions. Pittsburgh Pirates faithful are no exceptions.

Quite possibly, in an attempt to put these debates to rest, on September 18, 1999, the Pirates announced the results of balloting by fans for the "Team of the Century," following a two-month, write-in campaign in cooperation with the *Pittsburgh Post-Gazette*.

Receiving the most votes from the more than 14,000 fans who participated in the survey were: Bill Mazeroski (13,049), Roberto Clemente (12,791), Willie Stargell (12,579), and Honus Wagner (11,106).

The official results from the poll for the two highest numbers of votes for each position were:

First Base
Willie Stargell (12,579)
Dick Stuart (575)

Second Base
Bill Mazeroski (13,049)
Rennie Stennett (364)

Shortstop
Honus Wagner (11,106)
Dick Groat (951)

Third Base
Pie Traynor (9,754)
Bill Madlock (2,173)

Left Field
Ralph Kiner (7,948)
Barry Bonds (4,834)

Center Field
Lloyd Waner (4,726)
Andy Van Slyke (4,678)

Right Field
Roberto Clemente (12,791)
Paul Waner (890)

Catcher
Jason Kendall (5,508)
Manny Sanguillen (5,265)

Right-Handed Pitcher
Vernon Law (4,889)
Bob Friend (3,177)

Left-Handed Pitcher
Harvey Haddix (6,222)
John Candelaria (4,249)

Relief Pitcher
Kent Tekulve (6,366)
ElRoy Face (6,206)

Manager
Danny Murtaugh (7,875)
Jim Leyland (2,735)

Soon after the results of this vote were announced, the *Pittsburgh Post-Gazette* received an avalanche of phone calls from angry readers who disagreed with certain selections. Thus, the newspaper's goal to curb all debates went unfulfilled.

A curtain of gloom fell on the partisan crowd.

The once beautiful skies seemed to grow darker as the Yankees increased their lead by scoring two more runs in the eighth.

Behind 7–4, the Pirates could have shrugged their shoulders and accepted the fact that they did their best against incredible odds. But that was not the character of a team that had rallied to win 28 games that season when they trailed after the sixth inning. Pinch-hitter Gino Cimoli smacked a single. That seemed to be a wasted hit when Virdon hit a sure double-play grounder to short. The ball hit a pebble on the surface of the infield (which Manager Stengel later described as a "cabbage patch"), took a wicked hop, and caught shortstop Tony Kubek in the Adam's apple. Kubek lay prostrate on the ground, and both runners were ruled safe.

The blow sent a groggy Kubek to the hospital and proved to be a turning point. Groat's single made the game 7–5. Skinner's sacrifice bunt moved the tying run into scoring position. Two batters later, Roberto Clemente beat out a high chopper for an infield hit, and Virdon scored to bring the Pirates within one run.

Hal Smith, a reserve catcher who hit 11 home runs all year, stepped to the plate and, with one swing, etched his name into Pirates immortality. He sent a 1–2 pitch over the left-center-field wall for a home run, giving the Pirates a 9–7 lead.

The roar of the crowd may have registered a 7 on the Richter scale as radio broadcaster Chuck Thompson exclaimed, "Pittsburgh has just become an outdoor insane asylum. We have seen and shared in one of baseball's great moments."

Screaming fans and an announcer's hyperbole aside, the Yankees refused to surrender. Old reliable Bob Friend, in a rare relief appearance, yielded singles to Bobby Richardson and pinch-hitter Dale Long. After one out, Mantle singled off reliever Harvey Haddix, driving in a run. Berra then hit what appeared to be a double-play ball to Nelson at first base, but instead of throwing to second, Nelson chose to step on first, thus eliminating a force-out. Mantle dove back to first base, avoiding a tag as the tying run crossed the plate.

The stage was now set for the most dramatic ending in World Series history.

Leading off in the bottom of the ninth, with the score knotted at 9, Mazeroski faced new Yankees hurler Ralph Terry. The giant Longines clock high atop the scoreboard in left field showed the time as 3:36.

On a 1–0 count, Maz swung at a high fastball and sent it high and deep toward left field. Berra, playing left field, ran toward the wall and stopped. With his back facing the infield, the future Hall of Famer stood helplessly as he watched the 400-foot blast disappear into those outstretched limbs of trees in Schenley Park. Berra then fell to his knees, realizing that the ball and the World Series were out of his reach.

The 24-year-old Maz ran, skipped, and hopped around the bases, waving his hat over his head, his other arm windmilling in celebration. Some fans ran onto the field and followed him. The rest of Forbes Field erupted like a Bessemer converter at U.S. Steel. If it is true that baseball is life with the volume turned up, then Pittsburgh was living life to its fullest. For the next hour, according to *Sports Illustrated*, Forbes Field was awash in noise.

For the first time in 35 years, the Pirates were champions of the world and gave their fans a moment they would remember for the rest of their lives.

CLEMENTE: A TOUCH OF ROYALTY

Had ballet dancer Mikhail Baryshnikov elected to become a professional baseball player, he would have played right field like Roberto Clemente. Those fans fortunate enough to have seen Clemente during his 18-year career with the Pittsburgh Pirates saw artistry in motion whenever the flashy Puerto Rican outran a long fly ball or rifled a throw back to the infield.

During his rookie season in 1955, Clemente caught the attention of local fans not because of his overwhelming batting average (.255), but because of his unique way of playing the game. He shagged fly balls, for example, using a "basket catch," as did Willie Mays. When he tossed the ball back to the infield, he did so with a relaxed, underhanded motion that gave a disarming appearance of nonchalance. That abruptly changed during the game if an opposing base runner dared to challenge him to advancing from first to third on a hit to right field. Clemente's arm then became a howitzer, and the hapless runner slid into nothing but a ball awaiting him in the glove of a beaming third baseman.

Clemente took an unorthodox approach to hitting as well. When he stepped to the plate, he moved his shoulders around in tiny circles and twisted his body as would a person who had spent the entire night on a bad mattress. Constantly moving while in the batter's box, he often swung at pitches 10 inches outside the strike zone and laced them to right field for hits.

Pirates broadcaster Bob Prince became one of the media personalities who saw what most others missed—the raw material for a brilliant career. Prince, in fact, was chiefly responsible for creating a

The Great One made every play seem spectacular, especially when he stretched what would normally be a double into a triple.

special rallying cry for Clemente. Over the air he encouraged Pirates fans to holler "Arriba! Arriba!"—a cheer akin to the Spanish for *Rise up!*—whenever Clemente came to bat or performed one of his spectacular catches in right field.

Unfortunately, Prince and a few of the local sportswriters formed a small cheering section for the player who would later be identified as the Great One. Most experts today agree that had Clemente played in a major market and received the media attention that accompanies such venues, he would have earned many more national headlines.

During the 1960 season (the year the Bucs defeated the highly favored New York Yankees in the World Series), Clemente received due recognition from some of the national press. Some sportswriters went so far as to label Clemente as the most exciting player in baseball that year, as he hit a sizzling .314, with 16 home runs and a club-leading 94 RBIs.

Respected baseball insiders, such as writer Joe Falls of the *Detroit Free Press*, believed that Clemente wrote the book on how to play right field. Not only was he gifted with sure hands and gazelle-like quickness that reduced obvious extra-base hits to outs, but he also possessed a powerful throwing arm that gunned down many runners. "Clemente could field a ball in New York and throw a guy out in Pennsylvania," claimed veteran Dodgers broadcaster Vin Scully.

More than one visiting reporter sitting in the press box at Three Rivers Stadium confessed: "I would actually pay for a ticket just to see Roberto Clemente play right field."

That said, Clemente was still not given the accolades due to someone of his stature. Pittsburghers, of course, knew of his prowess. They appreciated the fact that Clemente played right field without a net, often forsaking potential harm to himself when he dove at low line drives or ran into a wall when chasing a fly ball.

As a demonstration of their love and admiration for him, on July 25, 1970, Pirates fans honored baseball's first Latin American superstar in a special ceremony before a home game. The famed right fielder returned their love and showed them how much he treasured the support of loyal fans: "I was born twice," he told the crowd. "I was born in 1934 and again in 1955 when I came to Pittsburgh. I am thankful I can say I had two lives."

Clemente's star shined brightest during the 1971 World Series between the Pirates and the Baltimore Orioles—known still as "the Clemente Series." It was perhaps the first time that all of the national media finally took note of the overflowing talent about which Pirates fans were already aware. The Pirates standout hit an astonishing .414 during the seven games of the Series and slugged two doubles, a triple, and two home runs. He also played a flawless right field with a confidence that bordered on arrogance. Jerry Izenberg, a writer for *The* (Newark) *Star-Ledger*, observed, "After 17 major league seasons, Roberto Clemente is an overnight sensation."

IT SHOULD HAVE BEEN OBVIOUS

Thirty-eight-year-old Frank Noah, a native Pittsburgher, was never what one might call a die-hard baseball fan. As a youngster, he had heard Pirates games being broadcast by Rosey Rowswell and Bob Prince on WWSW and later on KDKA radio. He knew something about the game, but he never developed a genuine passion for the sport. Noah, in fact, had never seen a Pirates game in person until one evening in 1972, when his Uncle Benny took him to Three Rivers Stadium to watch a contest between the Bucs and the St. Louis Cardinals. They had excellent seats—right behind home plate.

In the top half of the eighth inning, the Pirates were leading by one run. With only one out, Jose Cruz had just tripled for St. Louis and stood on third. The next hitter, Cardinals outfielder Lou Brock, lofted a fly ball to fairly deep right field into the waiting glove of Roberto Clemente. It looked like a routine sacrifice fly that would tie the game.

Cruz tagged up at third and took off for home in a gait somewhat slower than full speed. Big mistake. The large crowd rose to its feet and cheered in anticipation of what was going to happen. Clemente unleashed a bulletlike throw that reached catcher Manny Sanguillen on the fly. Even fans in the cheap seats could see the jovial Sanguillen's bright smile as he held the ball waiting to tag out the unsuspecting Cruz.

Home-plate umpire Harry Wendelstedt signaled the runner out, and Pirates fans screamed with delight.

Young Frank, still naïve to the finer points of baseball, turned to his uncle and asked, "Is that normal?"

"No," responded his Uncle Benny. "That was Clemente."

Clemente guaranteed his place in Cooperstown on September 30, 1972, when he slammed a double to left-center field at Three Rivers Stadium against the New York Mets. It was the 3,000th hit of his illustrious career. Baseball enthusiasts still remember the image of Clemente standing on second base, waving his hat in response to the five-minute standing ovation by the fans at the ballpark.

On the morning of January 1, 1973, no Pirates fan was in the mood to celebrate anything, including the New Year. Headlines in that morning's *Pittsburgh Post-Gazette* told the shocking story: "Clemente Dies in Plane Crash." Pittsburghers shook their heads in utter disbelief as they read news reports of how Clemente had volunteered to board a DC-7 aircraft the day before to help transport 16,000 pounds of relief supplies to earthquake victims in Managua, Nicaragua. Shortly after takeoff, the plane burst into flames, banked sharply to the left, and plunged deep into the ocean. Roberto Clemente was dead. No one ever found his body.

He was only 38 years old.

During his 18 years with the Pirates, Clemente topped the .300 mark 13 times, won four National League batting crowns, batted .317, hit 240 home runs, and knocked in 1,305 runs. He also won 12 Gold Glove awards for his outstanding fielding. He hit safely in all seven games of both the '60 and '71 World Series, winning the Series MVP award in '71. He was selected 12 times to the All-Star team and voted the National League MVP in 1966.

His epitaph on a memorial plaque in Puerto Rico reads: "I want to be remembered as a ballplayer who gave all he had to give."

When baseball commissioner Bowie Kuhn heard about the Pirates star's death, he described baseball's premier right fielder in just eight words: "He had about him a touch of royalty."

That was Roberto Clemente.

HOLY PIRATES

Among names of players who have worn the wool flannels or double-knits of the Pittsburgh Pirates, a few were members of the cloth or pillars of the church. Four of the more prominent ones follow:

Maximillian Carnarius "Max" Carey, who was recruited by Pirates scouts from a rather unusual venue. Carey wasn't a minor league standout. Instead, he was a second-year student on a seven-year track to become an ordained clergyman at the Concordia Lutheran College and Seminary in St. Louis.

He had planned on a ministerial career since childhood, but as he aged in years and athletic skills, he felt another call—this one from the gods of baseball. To the surprise of his professors and members of his home congregation in Terre Haute, Indiana, the 20-year-old calmly announced in late September 1910, "I came to the realization that baseball, rather than the holy ministry, was to be my life's work."

The scouts, who had kept a close eye on this fleet-footed prospect, immediately signed the young man, who exchanged a starched clerical collar for a baggy Pirates uniform. Carey justified the Pirates' faith in him when, at the tail end of the season, in just two games, he got three hits, including a triple, in six at-bats.

Carey would spend most of his 20-year career in Major League Baseball (1910–1929) with the Bucs. The switch-hitting outfielder batted over .300 with Pittsburgh six times and led the National League in stolen bases on 10 occasions. His best year was in 1925 as a member of the World Series championship team, when he hit a career-high .343 and led the league with 46 steals.

A few months into the 1926 season, things suddenly turned sour for the future Hall of Famer. Manager Bill McKechnie openly accused an injured Carey of not hustling. Carey responded by complaining to his teammates and to the press. By July 4, Carey and his manager were not speaking to each other. Owner Barney Dreyfuss sided with his manager, and Carey was released on waivers to Brooklyn on August 13.

Following his retirement as a player, Carey was instrumental in forming the All-American Girls Professional Baseball League in 1943. He managed the Milwaukee Chicks and the Fort Wayne Daisies of the league that was created to fill the gap left by disbanded minor league teams in World War II and made popular in recent years by the movie *A League of Their Own.*

Frank Joseph Thomas was a homegrown product of Pittsburgh who showed remarkable power at the plate. His ambition as a youth, however, was not to slam baseballs out of a stadium, but to win souls for his faith.

Thomas, a devout Roman Catholic, studied for the priesthood at the Mount Carmel College in Niagara Falls, Ontario.

As Max Carey had done before him, Thomas struggled with what his true calling in life should be. After much prayer and self-examination, he felt he had answered that question to the best of his ability. He left the seminary quietly and told his family, "I concluded that my calling was not to spend my professional life in front of an altar, but in front of baseball fans."

Thomas was signed by the only team he had ever followed—the Pittsburgh Pirates. The right-hand-hitting left fielder spent his first two years in the majors as a backup to local folk hero Ralph Kiner. "When Kiner was traded to Chicago in June 1953, I got my big break," remembers Thomas, who went on to lead his team that year with 30 home runs.

Plagued mostly with a poor supporting cast, Thomas was the only consistent long-ball hitter on clubs that seemed to struggle just to remain in the league. That changed in 1958 when Thomas went on a tear, leading the league in homers and knocking in nearly one run a game during the first half of the season. Now playing third base, Thomas, voted the Bucs' most popular player by the fans, tapered off during the second half of the year, but he and the Bucs surprised the baseball world when they finished in second place, eight games behind Milwaukee.

A three-time All-Star ('54, '55, and '58), Thomas played for 16 years with several teams, including the original 1962 Mets.

William Ashley "Billy" Sunday was anything but a religious zealot while playing with the Chicago White Stockings (forerunner of the Cubs). Like most of his fellow players, he loved baseball, booze, fighting, and women—not necessarily in that order.

During a day off in 1887, Sunday joined his teammates in some "serious beer drinking" at a variety of taverns in downtown Chicago. While he sat on a curb nursing a minor hangover, a small band of street musicians walked by playing some familiar hymns his mother used to sing to him as a child. Sunday was drawn to the band and visited a mission where, in his words, "I was converted and immediately gave up drinking and scarlet women."

Before the next season, Chicago swapped him to Pittsburgh, where he became the Pirates' regular center fielder.

A fan favorite, Sunday was a genuine draw during two mediocre campaigns in 1888 and 1889. He sparkled in the outfield and joined the league leaders in stolen bases. One reporter wrote, "The whole town is wild over Sunday."

In 1890, he was named team captain and became the Pirates' headline player. Unfortunately this was during one of the worst seasons in Pittsburgh history. Before the Bucs finished the year with a miserable 23–113 record, the team's front office ran out of money. In an act of desperation, the Pirates traded Sunday to the Philadelphia Phillies in August for $1,000 cash and two players.

Sunday played eight years in the big leagues, compiling a .248 average.

His real fame came afterward, when he launched crusades around the nation in portable tents with folding chairs and trails of sawdust. He drew literally thousands of people to his popular revivals at which he peppered fiery sermons with illustrations from the baseball diamond. Sometimes he would run across the stage in front of worshippers and slide into an imaginary home plate while shouting, "Safe!"

In his heyday, he preached against the demon called whiskey, employing the same degree of hyperbole. He promised to kick, punch, and bite the plague. "And when I'm old, and toothless, and fistless, and footless, I'll gum it to death until it goes home to perdition, and I go home to glory."

Vernon Sanders "Deacon" Law was an ordained deacon in the Church of Jesus Christ of Latter-day Saints, whose followers are commonly known as Mormons. Law, a Cy Young Award winner in 1960 after compiling a 20–9 season with a league-leading 18 complete games, served as unofficial team chaplain for the world champion Pirates that year. He offered a calming effect to manager Danny Murtaugh's team during the anxiety-ridden turmoil normally associated with ballclubs that vie for a pennant and a World Series win.

Unlike most of his teammates, this Idaho native never touched alcohol; he even eschewed drinking coffee and hot tea—a practice of his church.

Vernon "Deacon" Law was a benevolent individual, yet he was never afraid to challenge hitters who stood too close to the plate.

In spite of his devotion to things spiritual, Law was a rugged competitor. In 1955 against Milwaukee, the Deacon pitched 18 complete innings in a game that the Pirates eventually won in the nineteenth.

Opposing hitters testified that Law was not afraid to throw an occasional high, inside pitch in order to brush back someone standing too close to the plate. Nobody, however, can recall him ever purposely throwing at a hitter. Except one time.

During a heated contest with the Cubs in August 1960, the Chicago hurler plunked a Pirates hitter on the batting helmet. In

BY THE NUMBERS

1—The number of Pirates who have won the Baseball Writers Association of America Rookie of the Year Award (Jason Bay, 2004)

Note: Johnny Ray (1982) and Jason Kendall (1996) won *The Sporting News* Rookie of the Year Award.

the minds of everyone, especially Manager Murtaugh, this was a deliberate assault.

Murtaugh left his customary seat in the corner of the dugout to speak with Law, who was pitching for the Bucs that day. "I want you to throw at the head of the first guy who steps up to the plate just to send a message that we won't tolerate this kind of shit," ordered the salty Irishman.

"But, Skip," pleaded Law, "that would be against my religion. After all, the Bible says, 'Turn the other cheek.'"

Murtaugh wasn't impressed. "Let me put it this way. It'll cost you $500 if you don't knock him down."

Law paused for a second or two, then replied, "The Bible also says, 'He who lives by the sword shall also die by the sword.'"

Amen.

THE BAD

I f the word *fan* is an abbreviated form of the word *fanatic,* it means that the close follower of any baseball team (Pirates included) accepts the club in both good times and bad.

In examining some of the events and players who may not have left the best memories for us throughout the cold winter that follows the last day of a heart-breaking season, perhaps we can soothe our internal frustrations with the truth that the bad times make us appreciate even more the positive rewards granted by victories and stellar performances.

With that attempt to rationalize our disappointments, here are a few of the times in Pirates history that have left heads shaking in astonishment.

THE FIRST WORLD SERIES

The National League, still in its infancy in 1901, reluctantly recognized the upstart American League as an "equal rival." Truth be told, most club owners of National League teams refused to consider the "junior circuit" as anything but a minor league.

Their condescending attitude remained unchallenged for two full years; thus, there was no World Series pitting the best of one league against the other. The last time Major League Baseball came close to hosting a World Series was in 1900 when the National League's first-place Brooklyn Superbas played the second-place

Pirates in a best-of-five series for the Chronicle-Telegraph Cup (named after Pittsburgh's daily newspaper). An air of apathy engulfed the series won by Brooklyn, three games to one, all of which were played at Exposition Park in Pittsburgh before an average of slightly more than 2,000 fans per game.

Now that another league was regarded as an equal, American League president Ban Johnson, along with his spunky cohorts Charles Comiskey, Connie Mack, and Clark Griffith, adopted aggressive, antagonist tactics to woo some National League stars away from their teams. Their most successful ploy was to wave dollar signs before the eyes of players in a league that had a salary cap of $2,400. Some of the more famous names to jump ship were Napoleon Lajoie, Jimmy Collins, Denton "Cy" (short for "Cyclone") Young, and John McGraw. Pittsburgh lost two regulars in this mass exodus—infielder Jimmy Williams and catcher Harry Smith.

Pirates owner Barney Dreyfuss was particularly irritated by the manner in which he lost Williams. Dreyfuss had sent Williams money for train fare to transport him from his home in Denver to Hot Springs, Arkansas, site of the Pirates' training camp. On board the same train was John McGraw, now manager of the Baltimore franchise of the infant American League. McGraw huddled with the Pirates' third baseman and persuaded him to sign a contract with his club.

"What made me angry," recalled Dreyfuss, "was not only that I lost Williams, but that I paid for the train ticket so that McGraw could steal him."

Other Pittsburgh stars, including Honus Wagner, were vulnerable to the lure of higher paychecks by American League clubs, but they elected to remain loyal to Dreyfuss and Pirates manager Fred Clarke.

Tensions continued to simmer between the two leagues. That seething bitterness was part of the reason that no championship series was held in either 1901 or 1902.

Prior to Opening Day in 1903, the Pittsburgh Pirates appeared to be the best team in either league. The Pirates, however, played only average baseball at the start of the year and by the end of

May were in third place. The pressures apparently got the best of Manager Clarke, who volunteered to take a few days off beginning on the first of June to avoid suffering a nervous breakdown. If this was done to motivate the players, he could not have done a better job. Starting on June 2, Pirates pitchers began an amazing streak of six consecutive shutouts. A 15-game winning streak catapulted the Bucs into first place, where they remained until the end of the regular season. They eventually finished the year six and a half games ahead of the New York Giants.

Honus Wagner, who was persuaded to switch from right field to shortstop, not only flashed a slick glove in the field but also hit a lusty .355 to lead the senior circuit for the second time in four years. Player/manager Fred Clarke was not far behind, finishing second with an average of .351.

On the hill for the Pirates were Sam Leever (25–7 and a league-leading 2.06 ERA), Charles "Deacon" Phillippe (25–9, 2.43 ERA), and Ed Doheny (16–8, 3.19 ERA).

While the other owners of National League clubs were content to do battle with the rival American League, Dreyfuss elected to take another course of action. He saw much more value in using diplomacy and cooperating with owners of American League teams. Quite possibly, the real reason for his approach lay in the fact that he had the bulk of his finances tied up in his baseball club and he could not compete in a salary war to retain quality players.

Several weeks prior to the end of the 1903 season, when it became obvious that Pittsburgh would capture the National League title and the Boston Pilgrims would end the season as champions of the American League, Dreyfuss contacted Henry Killilea, president of the Boston club. The two of them discussed the possibility of staging a series of games between the two teams after the completion of the regular season.

Why would Pittsburgh agree to play against the winners of what was generally regarded as an inferior league? Some feel that Dreyfuss saw this as a way to gain extra revenue. Others credit him with a more altruistic motive, that is, to generate more harmony between the two leagues. Whatever the reason, both clubs agreed that they would stage a best-of-nine series they would call simply a championship series. It would later develop into what we know as the World Series.

In Game 1, held at the Huntington Avenue Grounds, home of the Pilgrims, a triple by Tommy Leach, followed by a run-scoring single by Honus Wagner off of legendary pitcher Cy Young, gave the impression that Pittsburgh truly outclassed Boston. That suspicion was confirmed when three more Pirates crossed the plate that same inning.

Pirates starter Deacon Phillippe yielded only goose eggs through six innings as the Pirates tacked on three more runs. The score was 7–0 before Boston got its first two runs in the seventh and added another meaningless run in the ninth. With the final score 7–3 in favor of Pittsburgh, it looked as though this would be a mighty short series.

In Game 2 fortunes reversed. Pirates starter Sam Leever complained of a sore arm and retired from the contest after the first inning, but not before Boston's Patsy Dougherty hit his first of two home runs that afternoon, helping pitcher Bill Dinneen to notch a 3–0 shutout.

That loss obviously got the attention of Clarke, who summoned Phillippe, with only one day's rest, to pitch Game 3 in Boston. Backed by timely doubles off the bats of Wagner, Clarke, Claude Ritchey, and Ed Phelps, the Pirates edged the Pilgrims, 4–2.

In the familiar surroundings of Exposition Park and holding a 2–1 lead in the series, Pittsburgh again called on its ace Phillippe, now with only two days' rest, to put another nail in the coffin of Boston in Game 4. Manager Clarke allowed himself to appoint Phillippe because of a rainout on the scheduled previous day.

The Deacon showed some understandable weariness, but he was able to squeak out a 5–4 win over Boston pitcher Dinneen. All the Pirates had to do now was win two more games, and the championship would be theirs.

Boston had another idea, as the immortal Cy Young limited the Bucs to six hits and a humiliating 11–2 loss in Game 5.

The Pirates, however, could not count on a big home-field advantage for the following game. A cavalcade of Boston fans

FEUDIN' AND FIGHTIN'

The Pirates were loaded with talent in 1903, yet the team was not immune to internal problems. One of them involved manager Fred Clarke and owner Barney Dreyfuss.

Clarke was a no-nonsense manager who never let anyone guess where he stood on a subject. His targets included umpires who he thought rendered wrong calls. His salty language on the field often embarrassed the very proper Dreyfuss, who, although a lifelong Jew, was really a Puritan at heart. While the chafing between the two men served as fodder for a few juicy stories in the press, it caused great concern for Dreyfuss.

Another incident making headlines involved one of the Pirates' star pitchers, Ed Doheny. Gifted with a blistering fastball and wicked curve, for some unexplained reason, Doheny developed a sore arm in July. His ailing arm failed to respond to treatment, and the pitcher grew despondent. Over the next few weeks and months, his normal, upbeat approach to life eroded into anger with himself. He was unable to pitch the rest of the year.

The frustrations mounted to such an extent that just prior to the end of the season, Doheny went on a rampage around the clubhouse. While cursing, screaming, and swinging his arms at anything or anyone around him, the erratic southpaw had to be subdued by his teammates. Police were called to escort him out of the locker room. Eventually he was confined to a mental hospital near his home in Danvers, Massachusetts.

The story does not have a happy ending. Doheny didn't respond to treatment. Instead, within the first few weeks at the hospital, he physically assaulted a nurse and a physician. He remained a patient in the Danvers institution until he died 13 years later.

journeyed to Pittsburgh with the team. Included in the ensemble was a brass band dubbed the Royal Rooters, who were unafraid to make as much noise as possible and turn the venue into a home-field advantage for the Pilgrims.

The Royal Rooters played loud and long as the Pilgrims' Bill Dinneen showed that he, too, was an "iron man." In his third trip to the mound in just eight days, he bested the sore-armed Leever in Game 6 by a score of 6–3.

Pittsburgh and the National League grew nervous. With the series tied at three games apiece, neither organization could stand the thought of losing to an American League franchise.

Still in Pittsburgh for Game 7, pitcher Phillippe got a welcomed extra day's rest due to a rain delay. He probably needed more time, however, as the Pilgrims defeated him and the Pirates handily, 7–3, on a slippery field.

Weather conditions were not much better in Boston for Game 8. Another scheduled game day was washed out. That provided a window of opportunity for Deacon Phillippe again to take the mound for what became an all-time record fifth start in any World Series. His opponent was, as might be expected, Bill Dinneen, who was about to make his fourth appearance.

With Pittsburgh unwilling to believe that this could be happening to them, and Boston eager to prove they could compete with the best in the National League, tensions between the two clubs rose to a fever pitch. That became evident when Fred Clarke laid a bunt down the first-base line. Boston's first baseman George "Candy" LaChance fielded the ball. He attempted a quick throw to first to catch the speedy Clarke but, instead, hit the Pirates manager in the back. Irate players bolted from their respective dugouts; even some fans ran onto the field. Umpires Tommy Connolly and Hank O'Day spent the next half-hour restoring order.

The Deacon pitched quite well once the game resumed, allowing only three runs the entire game. Dinneen did better, shutting out the Pirates on only four hits.

The unthinkable had happened. The champions of the neophyte American League had defeated the powerful Pittsburgh Pirates.

In a gesture of appreciation to his players not only for their efforts in bringing a National League championship to Pittsburgh, but also because of their loyalty to him while others jumped to the American League, Dreyfuss added his club owner's share of the proceeds to the players' pool, giving each Pirate $1,316.25. It was the only time in history that players of the losing team took home more Series money than players for the winning squad. There's a "P.S." to the story. The next year, undoubtedly because of the humiliation suffered by the Pirates following the 1903 season, after his New York Giants won the National League crown, Giants president John Brush refused to engage in any series of games with those he labeled as "minor leaguers." Alas, there was no World Series in 1904.

WHEN THE PIRATES LOST THE WORLD SERIES IN BATTING PRACTICE

Many historians mark 1927 as a turning point in America for a variety of reasons.

In aviation, the year marked the first solo flight across the Atlantic Ocean—accomplished by a pilot named Charles Augustus Lindbergh. As a result, he became an international symbol of bravery and endurance, and the greatest folk hero ever to climb into a cockpit.

At Chicago's Soldier Field, the legendary Jack Dempsey nearly regained his heavyweight belt when he floored the champion, Gene Tunney, in the seventh round but failed to go to a neutral corner during the famed "long count."

Baseball fans recall this year as the one in which the New York Yankees' George Herman "Babe" Ruth set the home-run mark of 60 in 154 games. That milestone would remain for 34 years until another Yankee, Roger Maris, surpassed it during a 162-game schedule.

Many baseball experts still regard those 1927 Yankees of Babe Ruth as the best team ever assembled on a baseball diamond. Sluggers such as Ruth and Lou Gehrig, along with other big guns in the arsenal—Tony Lazzeri, Bob Meusel, and Earle Combs—enabled the lineup dubbed Murderers' Row by the press to waltz to an American League–leading 110–44 record, a whopping 19 games ahead of the second-place Philadelphia Athletics.

Facing the mighty Yankees in the World Series that year was another group of players who were anything but pushovers. The 1927 Pittsburgh Pirates posed a formidable lineup of their own.

Many astute observers feel that had Kiki Cuyler been allowed to play in the 1927 World Series, the Bucs would not have dropped four-straight games to the New York Yankees.

Although they lacked the long-ball power of the Yankees (the entire team belted only 54 homers for the season, and the team leaders were Glenn Wright and Paul Waner with 9), they did have future Hall of Famers Harold "Pie" Traynor, Paul and Lloyd Waner, Joe Cronin (who played in only 12 games that year), and Hazen Shirley "Kiki" Cuyler. The team impressed most of the nation's sportswriters, who predicted during spring training that the Pirates would run away with the National League pennant.

However, internal strife among the Bucs that year—especially between manager Donie Bush and fan-favorite Cuyler—was enough of a distraction to cause the Bucs to struggle in their quest for the crown. At the end of the regular season, the Pirates were fortunate to win the championship by only one and a half games over St. Louis.

Nonetheless, the baseball world was set on seeing the results of the matchup between these two talented teams.

The surprising dimension to this World Series was not that one squad outhit or outpitched the other. Instead, the Series was lost before the first pitch was tossed.

Let's look at two important dimensions.

First, the Pirates could not hope to win the world championship by going head-to-head in a home-run-hitting contest. Even the most casual fan of that era realized that the Yanks completely dominated in that area. If they were going to prevail, the Pirates had to pitch well and eke out runs by playing "small ball," that is, hit singles and an occasional double, steal bases, execute hit-and-run plays, and capitalize on breaks.

The fastest runner on the squad was Cuyler. Although he spent nearly half the season on the bench, he led the Bucs with 20 stolen bases along with batting a healthy .309 and was generally regarded as the team's most complete player.

Why would Cuyler, who was not injured, spend so much time watching the games from the dugout? It was due to a spat between him and his manager.

The talented Pirates seemed to lack enthusiasm for the game in the mind of Manager Bush. In addition, Cuyler was in the midst of a rare slump. To ignite a fire under his players, Bush juggled the lineup, moving Cuyler from his customary third slot to batting second.

On the first day of the new lineup, Cuyler went 0-for-5.

Cuyler complained to Bush. The manager's unsympathetic response was, "You'll get used to it."

Tensions increased over the next few games as Cuyler continued to give poor showings. "Take me out of the second slot before I become the worst player on the team," demanded Cuyler.

Bush stood his ground even more firmly. "You'll stay there until I'm ready to change you," he promised.

A few days later when Cuyler failed to slide into second base in an effort to break up a double play, Bush fined the gifted outfielder $25.

Local sportswriters played up the bitterness between the two; most of them sided with Cuyler.

Perhaps to show both his players and the press who was boss, Bush benched Cuyler in favor of the much slower outfielder Clyde Barnhart, not only for the remainder of the season but for the entire World Series as well.

The second factor in losing the Series had much more to do with psychology than physical skills.

Joe Cronin, who would become a Hall of Famer after moving to the American League, was a backup on the Pirates that season. Until his death in 1984, he delighted in telling the story of how the Yankees' Ruth—a master at creating a psychological advantage—got an idea during the pregame warm-ups. Just before stepping into the batter's box, Ruth asked the batting practice pitcher to throw the ball at medium speed, right down the middle of the plate, belt-high. The pitcher did as Ruth wanted. On his very first swing, the Bambino propelled the ball on a line drive deep into the second tier of the right-field stands at Forbes Field.

Pittsburgh players, some of whom were heading for the clubhouse to change uniforms, heard the ball rattling around the second-deck seats. They stopped in their tracks to watch with reverence.

Ruth lined the second pitch into the lower deck.

On his third swing, he sent the ball even deeper into the second tier than the first.

On the fourth pitch, Ruth took a tumultuous swing that would have made Paul Bunyan proud. He sent the ball high and deep, a prodigious shot that hit the façade of the roof. No one before had hit a ball that hard in Forbes Field.

Ruth chuckled under his breath and nodded to his teammate, Lou Gehrig, inviting him to take a few swings. The Iron Horse, as they called him, responded by sending the first pitch over the right-field screen about 10 rows back in the first deck.

"Good, but not excellent," chided Ruth. His remark was aimed not at Gehrig, but at the Pirates who stood silent and in awe.

Lloyd Waner broke the silence of the team when he turned to his manager and said, "Geeze, they're big, aren't they?" Manager Bush, with a sigh that showed more than a hint of apprehension, responded, "Let's get out onto the ball field and just hope we don't all get killed."

The Pirates put on a surprisingly good showing in both games in Pittsburgh and the remaining contests in New York. At the end, however, it was all for naught as the Pirates lost the Series in a four-game sweep.

Could it be possible that the Pittsburgh Pirates really lost the 1927 World Series in batting practice?

STORMY WEATHER

The 1938 season for the Pittsburgh Pirates must be engraved in baseball's archives as one of the most frustrating for Pirates players, management, and fans. Overflowing with raw talent and solid experience, the '38 version of the Bucs was the odds-on favorite among Depression-era gamblers to capture the National League crown. Their prediction was confirmed when the Pirates catapulted out of the starting gate with warp-speed success, winning their first seven games with relative ease.

Manager Pie Traynor, along with the rest of the Pirates faithful, delighted in the performance of a young rookie outfielder, Johnny Rizzo, whom the team recently picked up from the

St. Louis Cardinals' farm team in Columbus. The Italian native of Houston clubbed 23 home runs that year, more than any Pirate before him.

Other notable hitters were outfielders Lloyd "Little Poison" Waner (.313, five home runs), his brother Paul "Big Poison" Waner (whose .280 average and six home runs resulted in an off year by his standards), and shortstop Joseph "Arky" Vaughan (.322, seven homers). All three would later be enshrined in the Baseball Hall of Fame.

The mound staff included Bob Klinger (12–5, 2.99 ERA) and one of the game's first respected relief specialists, Mace "Fireman" Brown (13–9, 3.80 ERA).

Beginning on June 1, and throughout the sweltering heat of a Pittsburgh summer, the team compiled a 40–15 record, including a 13-game winning streak. The Bucs looked nearly unbeatable, said the experts, including those in other National League cities. After his New York Giants had just lost three of four games to the Pirates, manager Bill Terry raised a white flag when he told reporter Charles J. "Chilly" Doyle of the *Pittsburgh Sun-Telegraph,* "If these Pirates don't win the pennant, they should quit playing ball."

The Pirates' domination of the league continued through September 1, when the Bucs posted a comfortable seven-game lead over the second-place Chicago Cubs, a team that was hampered by internal problems. In a last-gasp effort to turn things around in August, Chicago abruptly fired its popular manager, Charlie Grimm, and replaced him with their catcher, Charles "Gabby" Hartnett, assigning him the role as player/manager.

Back at Forbes Field, Pirates owner Bill "Bensy" Benswanger, anticipating that a World Series would come to the Steel City, ordered the construction of an additional press box in the third deck above home plate. This was no small project. The new facility could seat 600 visiting reporters who were certain to come from cities throughout the nation to cover the 1938 fall classic.

While carpenters' hammers pounded nails in Forbes Field, 520 miles to the west in Wrigley Field, Chicago Cubs bats were smacking baseballs at a remarkable clip. Hartnett appeared to be the

BY THE NUMBERS

1—Pirates in the elite "30/30 Club"—Barry Bonds, who hit 33 home runs and stole 52 bases in 1990

right man for the right time. He and his Cubs, nearly unnoticed by the national media, inched their way toward the top of the standings.

In mid-September, during the last two weeks of the season, the Pirates battled not only other teams, but also the weather. A 95 mph hurricane lashed New York, Philadelphia, and Boston during the team's last swing through the eastern seaboard, knocking out four games against the seventh-place Brooklyn Dodgers and last-place Philadelphia Phillies. League rules at that time prohibited the games from being made up.

The next stop on the Bucs' road trip was Wrigley Field for a crucial three-game series against a fired-up Cubs team that was now only one and a half games behind Pittsburgh.

In Game 1, former Cardinal Jay Hanna "Dizzy" Dean, who would win only seven games for the Cubs that season, reached deep inside himself to pitch a masterful 2–1 victory.

Leading by a mere half-game, the Pirates now faced a must-win situation. On a gloomy afternoon, with dark clouds hovering overhead and a thick haze creeping into Wrigley—a ballpark that would not get lights for another 50 years—the Bucs gained confidence when Rizzo slammed his 21st homer of the year, and third baseman Lee "Jeep" Handley came through with a clutch bases-loaded single giving Pittsburgh a 5–3 lead going into the bottom half of the eighth. That optimism waned as Chicago rallied for two runs to knot the contest. The outlook for the Pirates grew as bleak as the weather when they failed to score in the top of the ninth.

The three umpires gathered at home plate and determined the weather was so bad that if the Cubs failed to score in the home half of the inning, they would declare the game a tie.

HOW WET WAS IT?

Playing conditions in the early part of the 20th century were clearly not as favorable as today's modern surfaces. Astute groundskeepers with sophisticated equipment such as rollaway tarps and properly engineered draining systems have contributed to making playing fields much safer for the players.

That was not necessarily the case in 1903 when the Pittsburgh Pirates had to play at Exposition Park, located on the site of a Three Rivers Stadium parking lot. It was a massive field—400 feet down the lines and 450 feet to dead center. Home runs, consequently, were at a premium.

What was not scarce, however, was water, especially when the banks of the Allegheny River overflowed following a torrential downpour. In addition, right field sloped slightly downhill from the infield. When the onrushing water from the river flooded the field, players were sometimes required to play ankle-deep in water.

A special ground rule was employed during these times. Any ball hit into the flooded area was ruled a single, and base runners could advance only one base.

That appeared to be the fate of the contest when pitcher Mace Brown quickly retired the first two Cubs batters. Hartnett, the final hope for Chicago that afternoon, stepped to the plate, unable to see Pirates left fielder Rizzo because of the haze that resembled the sort of brownish-gray smog normally associated with smokestacks at the Homestead Works back in Pittsburgh.

Brown tossed two sharp-breaking curveballs for strikes. With the count 0–2, Brown tried to slip another curve past the burly catcher. Big mistake. Hartnett swung and connected with an ear-shattering *crack!* Both Hartnett and Brown knew the ball was gone, although neither could see it; the gray fog that engulfed Wrigley Field obscured the flight of the blast. Only the roar of the partisan crowd in the left-field bleachers told the story. It was a game-winning home run. The so-called Homer in the Gloamin' catapulted the Cubs over the Pirates and into first place.

The disheartened Pirates, now trailing Chicago by a half-game, must have felt as if the gods of baseball were toying with them. That suspicion was confirmed the next afternoon as Chicago clobbered Pittsburgh, 10–1.

The Cubs eventually won the National League pennant, ending the season two games ahead of the second-place Pirates.

To his dying day, owner Benswanger blamed the Pirates' demise not so much on Hartnett's homer but on the hurricane that had canceled four games a week earlier. "The pennant was lost *before* the Cubs series," he insisted. "The hurricane prevented us from winning. We went east good and hot. Everybody knows that when a club is hot, it can make wrong plays and still win; when it's cold, nothing turns out right. Losing ballgames is one thing; to lose by idleness is another."

After the Chicago Cubs lost the 1938 World Series in a four-game sweep to Joe DiMaggio and his New York Yankees, those brand-new press box seats high above the playing surface at Forbes Field would not hold World Series reporters for another 22 years.

WHAT'S IN A NAME?

One of the most frightening experiences for any Major League Baseball player is his first at-bat while wearing a big-league uniform. None, however, could be as confusing as the first trip to the plate by a little-known rookie outfielder for the Pittsburgh Pirates named Everitt Little Booe. His last name was pronounced with a silent "e," sounding like the common exclamation for Halloween: "*Boo!*"

For the record, Booe would play one season (1913) for the Pirates, and for Indianapolis and Buffalo of the Federal League.

Booe's unforgettable initial at-bat was during spring training in 1913 as a pinch-hitter. Before the young man left the dugout, Pirates manager Fred Clarke reminded him to announce his name to the home-plate umpire and future Hall of Famer Bill Klem. Spring-training ballparks in those days were not equipped with sophisticated public address systems, so umpires had to shout to the opponent's dugout and to the fans the name of any new player entering the contest.

The rookie, eager to make a good impression, grabbed a bat, ran toward the batter's box, and stood behind Klem, who was bent over, dusting off the plate with the customary whisk broom.

"Booe!" exclaimed the rookie to the umpire.

Klem stopped sweeping, slowly turned his head, and looked up over his shoulder with a scowl on his face. "What'd you say, kid?"

"Booe!" replied the rookie, this time a bit louder. "I said, 'Booe'!"

"Listen, kid," screamed Klem, who now stood nose-to-nose with the nervous player. "This ain't no joke. If you try to make a fool outta me one more time, I'm gonna kick you outta this f*cking game." Saliva mixed with tobacco juice spewed from the arbiter's mouth as his voice increased in volume. "Ya got that straight? Now, very slowly, just tell me yer name!"

The puzzled rookie was beside himself. Thinking that the veteran umpire may have lost some of his hearing, he stepped back, took a deep breath, and shouted to the top of his lungs, "BOOE!" For emphasis, he repeated his name. "BOOE!"

"Okay, kid, you asked for it. Yer outta here," Klem growled as he pointed straight to the Pirates' bench.

Seeing what was happening, Clarke and his star outfielder Max Carey ran from the dugout to the home-plate area and explained to Klem the reason for the misunderstanding.

Klem listened patiently, then agreed to permit the youngster to bat. But before he resumed his position behind the plate, Klem paused, looked squarely into the eyes of the now-relieved rookie, and said, "Kid, if you ever expect to stay in this league, you better change yer f*cking name."

THE UGLY

In the saga of any organization, as in every family, there are moments or people we might feel are best left forgotten. If so, that would be a mistake. Whether we are willing to admit it, even from these not-so-endearing memories come the fabric with which we weave our rich history.

Would America's fight for independence be as meaningful without the willingness of brave colonists to give the ultimate sacrifice during the Revolutionary War? Would Martin Luther King Jr.'s sacrifices for civil rights be as heroic were it not for the evils of slavery and mob lynching?

Likewise, the "ugly" parts of baseball—i.e., those bad instances that have been allowed to grow out of proportion—give us a taste of what the sport could be like were it not for the wisdom and leadership of those willing to stand up for what they knew was the right thing to do.

In this spirit, we present these rather unpleasant, yet (hopefully) meaningful, bits of Pirates history.

A DRUG SCANDAL ROCKS PITTSBURGH

The illegal use of drugs among Major League Baseball players did not begin with today's headlines about power hitters injecting themselves with human growth hormone and other steroids. As early as the 1980s, some baseball players who earned exorbitant

37

HOW BAD WERE THEY?

Catcher Joe Garagiola spent nine seasons in the big leagues, mostly with the St. Louis Cardinals. But from 1951 to 1953 he played in 217 games with the Pittsburgh Pirates. This included the entire 1952 campaign with the team tagged as the "Rickey Dinks."

Garagiola's .257 lifetime batting average and 42 career home runs did not make him a genuine prospect for the Hall of Fame as a player. He did, however, become enshrined in 1991 as winner of the Ford C. Frick Award for broadcasters.

Part of Garagiola's on-air charm was his quick wit. His willingness to look at baseball from a humorous dimension resulted in his becoming a popular after-dinner speaker and the author of the best-selling book *Baseball Is a Funny Game*.

That lighthearted perspective served him well when he played for the infamous 1952 Pirates club. "We had to laugh, otherwise we'd cry," he said.

Here are just a few of the other observations he made about the team:

"We finished in last place...on merit."

"Sometimes fans left a game early. That was not surprising. But when they left by walking across the infield—while we were still on it—that was disturbing to the players."

"During the seventh inning of one of our night games, our shortstop once dropped an easy, infield pop fly. His excuse afterward was, 'I lost it in the moon.'"

"I swear, some of our players must have held a secret meeting prior to each game and created new ways to lose a ballgame."

"The 1952 Pirates were so bad, when we had a rainout, we held a victory dance."

"We gave the fans their money's worth. They always saw the bottom of the ninth."

"We'd be a couple of runs behind before they finished playing the National Anthem."

"Opposing pitchers would get into fistfights over who was going to start against us."

salaries elected to spend some of their money on cocaine and similar substances.

The primary venue for this sordid activity in 1985 was the clubhouse of the Pittsburgh Pirates at Three Rivers Stadium. The cast of characters in this rather bizarre plot included some players (one of whom many regarded as a superstar), a local drug dealer, and the dealer's best friend, the Pirates' mascot.

Dale Shiffman, a native Pittsburgher, grew up with his pal Kevin Koch. "We were as close as brothers," said Shiffman. That closeness never waned until a betrayal not only ruined their friendship but also threatened to destroy the sport and the team they loved.

Like most young baseball fans, both Shiffman and Koch dreamed of one day becoming major league ballplayers. Koch was closest to fulfilling that fantasy when he attended a Pirates tryout camp. Unfortunately, he never possessed enough talent to attract the eyes of the scouts. Still, he yearned somehow to be a part of the team.

He saw an opportunity to do just that in 1978 when an ad appeared in the *Pittsburgh Post-Gazette* calling for auditions as the Pirates' mascot. This was not a path he had envisioned for himself as a young boy playing sandlot ball in Pittsburgh, but Koch slipped into the bulky green-and-yellow costume of the Parrot and went through a series of gyrations. "Apparently, it was good enough to impress the judges," he said. "Two weeks later they called and told me I was their guy.

"When I became the Parrot, I felt I had become part of the team. Not just any team. This was 1979. It was the 'Fam-A-Lee' with Willie Stargell, Tim Foli, John Candelaria, Kent Tekulve, and big Dave Parker. I felt I had died and gone to heaven."

Koch invited his boyhood chum Shiffman, a freelance photographer, into the clubhouse to mingle with the players. Shiffman, a gregarious type, quickly became friends with some of them—and even shagged fly balls during batting practice. "I got to stand out there in right field with my heroes," Shiffman recalled. "A few would even invite me to meet after the game to have a beer. Life could not have been better."

This was a great time for anyone associated with the Pirates. The 1979 squad embodied everything that was good about baseball. This small-market team captured the imagination of Americans when it won not only the National League pennant, but also the World Series to the beat of a song recorded by a disco quartet, Sister Sledge, titled "We Are Family."

The city of Pittsburgh joined in the chorus. It was a time to celebrate, especially for those closest to the team.

Players were met in every city by starry-eyed groupies known as "Baseball Annies." "Even *I* was able to 'bed' and drink anything I wanted," admitted Koch.

As years went by, those wild times included other highly questionable activities, including the use of cocaine.

"It was out there," remembered Dave Parker. "It was the thing to do at the time. People gravitated to athletes. All you had to do was ask for something and you got it."

Among his teammates who were also snorting cocaine were infielder Dale Berra and pitcher Rod Scurry. Scurry once went searching for cocaine during the late innings of a Pirates game.

When players wanted to score some drugs, they didn't have to go far. Shiffman knew several dealers in the neighborhood. He arranged with his dear friend Koch—the Pirate Parrot—to be his point man inside the clubhouse. It started slowly at first; then the orders increased. It was a simple formula for success. Shiffman supplied the cocaine; Koch delivered it.

For Parker this was merely a recreational activity, but it became much more for others as Parker was soon to find out. "I got a call about 4:00 one morning that I should contact Dale Berra right away and urge him to get help. I immediately telephoned him and learned that he had been clawing through canisters in his apartment in a near panic trying to find some cocaine."

Rumors circulated throughout Major League Baseball that key players on several teams were involved with the illegal substance. Those whispers caught the ear of Wells Morrison, a resident agent in the FBI's Monongahela Valley office near Pittsburgh. His investigation, as it turned out, was relatively easy. "Most every ballplayer

---

WHEN THE WALLS DID NOT COME TUMBLING DOWN

Perhaps in an attempt to re-create the famous biblical story about the prophet Joshua who marched around the city of Jericho and watched as the walls came tumbling down, the management of the Pittsburgh Pirates attempted to remove the left-field wall when the times called for it.

On June 4, 1953, when Branch Rickey traded away the Pirates' powerful home-run king, Ralph Kiner, he ordered the ground crew to tear down the structure in left field known as Greenberg Gardens and later Kiner's Korner, thus increasing the distance to the left-field wall from 335' to its original 365'.

When he caught wind of this proposed change, however, baseball commissioner Ford Frick immediately telephoned Rickey and ordered him to keep the structure intact until the end of the season.

---

to whom I spoke identified other players. Many of the users were All-Stars."

The agents then spoke with Scurry, a journeyman pitcher in his sixth year with the club. He revealed names of teammates who he knew, firsthand, were users.

Agent Morrison faced a dilemma. As a Pittsburgher, he was a fan of the Pirates. At the same time, he had a sworn duty to uphold. He wanted to get the job done as quickly as possible. He went right to the source—Kevin Koch. Realizing that the FBI had all the hard evidence needed to send both him and Shiffman away for many years, Koch agreed to cooperate fully. He volunteered to be wired and to record the next drug transaction with his best friend.

On May 31, 1985, at 6:30 in the morning, two federal agents knocked on the door of the South Hills home of Shiffman. Armed with warrants for his arrest, they placed him in handcuffs. On the local evening news, KDKA-TV's Bill Burns narrated the scandalous story over pictures of Shiffman being hauled away to jail.

"That was the worst day of my life," confessed Shiffman, "until the next afternoon. It was then my attorney told me that it was my best friend—Kevin Koch—who set me up."

I GUESS HE MEANT NO

With a record of 42–112 and a last-place finish, the 1952 Pirates could have been arrested for impersonating a Major League Baseball team. The only bright spot in the entire season was the fact that slugger Ralph Kiner led the National League in home runs (37) for the seventh consecutive year.

Before spring training Kiner met with general manager Branch Rickey to sign a new contract. He was shocked to discover that the new contract included a 25 percent cut from his previous year's $90,000 salary.

Seldom did Kiner ever express resentment, but this was just too much to take without protest.

"Why am I cut 25 percent?" he asked. "I led the league in home runs last year."

Rickey took the trademark cigar from his mouth, raised one of his bushy eyebrows, and asked, "Where did we finish last year?"

"Ahhhhh, in last place, Mr. Rickey," responded Kiner, uncertain where the general manager was heading with his question.

"Hummmm," said Rickey. "Well, son, let me tell you something. We could've finished in last place without you."

As the story began to unfold about the huge number of players involved in the scandal, Tom Brokaw of NBC, Dan Rather of CBS, and other national newscasters joined in the litany of despair. Rather's unsteady voice reflected his disappointment when he reported that the latest developments have "all of the drama of a tense ballgame."

Lonnie Smith of the Cardinals, Keith Hernandez of the Mets, and Dave Parker, now with the Cincinnati Reds, were among the most prominent names. In testimonies to a grand jury, each owned up to the accusations against him. In all, 21 players were implicated.

Reaction around the nation was mixed. In Pittsburgh, fans expressed outrage at Berra and Scurry and turned their backs on the team, with only 735,900 fans going through the Three Rivers Stadium turnstiles. Meanwhile, during his first at-bat with the

Mets following the revelations, Hernandez received a standing ovation.

None of the players would receive suspensions from baseball commissioner Peter Ueberroth or jail time from legal authorities if they agreed to donate a small percentage of their 1986 salaries to a drug program and perform community service. Shiffman, on the other hand, was indicted on 111 counts, pled guilty to 20, and was eventually sentenced in 1991 to 12 years in prison. He served 24 months.

From the day he was arrested, including his time behind bars, he never communicated with his former friend, Kevin Koch. Koch, because of the public outcry against him for what he had done, had quietly slipped out of the Pittsburgh area to live in California.

Shiffman at first was bitter. "I didn't believe that I would get the jail sentence. I was wondering why these guys got away with a slap on the wrist." That soon changed. "God got my attention," he said. "I'm not preaching at you. I'm just telling you the truth."

Shiffman, at that time, did not know how lucky he was. He now believes if he had continued on the path he'd been on, "I'd probably be dead with all the drugs and drinking."

As difficult as it may be for any of us to comprehend, Shiffman completely forgave his old friend for turning him in.

Sportscaster Bryant Gumbel, in a September 2006 episode of HBO's *Real Sports*, presented a moving story of how both Shiffman and Koch reunited after 13 years. Shiffman drove to Koch's California home, and the two embraced warmly. Shiffman's willingness to forgive had overcome all the anger.

"That was amazing," said Koch. "Pieces of my heart were shattered."

Both men have since steered clear of trouble and have solid jobs. Nonetheless, neither can ever get away completely from his past. Koch remembers picking up a copy of the history of the Pirates and seeing his name and the story of how the two of them "were up to their necks in the middle of it."

Although no players ever missed a game because of their drug-related activities, there were other lingering consequences for some.

Parker posted what some experts deem to be Hall of Fame numbers, although if he ever hopes to be enshrined, he will have to overcome this hurdle from his past. To this day, he feels his admission has poisoned the voters against him.

Berra remained a part-time player following his trials and was out of Major League Baseball after two years.

Scurry was traded to the Yankees in 1985 and lasted three more years in the game. He continued to battle his cocaine habit with no success. Finally, in a small hotel room in Reno, Nevada, in 1992, he was found dead from a drug-related incident. Rodney Grant Scurry was only 36 years old.

THE "RICKEY DINKS"

There's an adage used often during hard times: "I complained when I had no shoes, until I saw a man with no feet."

Pirates fans who lived (and suffered) during the early 1950s can identify with that saying. It matters not how bad a record any current era of Pirates might be, because nothing could compare with the ineptness of the teams from 1949 to 1955. Those who remained loyal to the Bucs during that period deserve diamond-studded medals of valor.

Pittsburgh had just completed a promising season in 1948 when two players—Stan Rojek and Danny Murtaugh—joined the squad to solidify shortstop and second base. Fine pitching performances by rookie Bob Chesnes, plus veterans Elmer Riddle and Rip Sewell, combined with the long-ball hitting of Ralph Kiner (a league-leading 40 home runs) and Wally Westlake (17 homers), had local fans daring to dream of a pennant. That year the Pirates actually led the league for a while before running out of steam and achieving a fourth-place finish. It was enough to cause the Pittsburgh faithful to look with eager anticipation toward next year.

Despite the fact that Kiner led the league in home runs during the next two campaigns (54 in 1949 and 47 in 1950), the Pirates finished those seasons in sixth and eighth (last) place, respectively. Billy Meyer, named National League Manager of the Year in

The author of the infamous Rickey Dinks of 1952 was the Bucs' general manager, Branch Rickey.

1948, was now just another ho-hum skipper with a team that showed little promise to win the coveted title again.

Something drastic had to be done.

Pirates owner John Galbreath took a bold step and lured Branch Rickey away from the Brooklyn Dodgers to be his general manager. Considered a shrewd and courageous baseball man, Rickey was one of the people most responsible for bringing Jackie Robinson into the big leagues. This Bible-quoting graduate of Ohio Wesleyan and the University of Michigan Law School had crossed swords with some of the other owners of the Dodgers, who persuaded him to sell his 25 percent share of the team.

Galbreath quickly brought him into the Pirates fold to turn things around for Pittsburgh.

Shortly following a warm reception by Pirates owners, the local press, and loyal fans, Rickey announced that he had a five-year plan designed to bring a pennant to the Steel City. That plan included getting rid of veteran players and bringing in young-sters—some right out of high school—who had little professional experience.

With Kiner as his only "name" player, Rickey offered contracts to local athletes such as pitchers Ron Kline and Ron Necciai, first baseman Tony Bartirome, and outfielders Bobby Del Greco, Brandy Davis, and Paul Smith. Others on the Pirates rosters during the 1951, 1952, and 1953 seasons were those who will be remembered only by the most die-hard fans. The lineups featured the likes of Jack Phillips, George Strickland, Paul LaPalme, Toby Atwell, Ted Beard, Woody Main, George Metkovich, Pete Castiglione, Jack Merson, and Clem Koshorek.

Some bright spots emerged from this collection of players. Kiner led the league in home runs each of the seasons for the fifth, sixth, and seventh years in a row, setting a record that probably

A "DOCTOR" IN THE HOUSE

Appearing in 19 games for the infamous 1952 Pirates was John "Bernie" Berardino, a second baseman in his 11th and final season in the major leagues.

Although he had racked up some decent statistics with the St. Louis Browns during the years of World War II, the strikingly handsome athlete of Italian heritage was not the answer to the Pirates' problems in '52 as he batted only .143 with no home runs.

Berardino's meteoric rise to national prominence came not on the base-ball field, but instead in front of a television camera. For 25 years, he was the heartthrob of women throughout America when he played the role of Dr. Steve Harvey on TV's General Hospital.

will never be broken. A young outfielder, Gus Bell, showed some pop from the left side of the plate but was sent to the minors because Rickey was convinced that he broke training rules when Bell elected to tend to his ill wife instead of playing in a few games during spring training.

Pitcher Murry Dickson would win 20 games in '51, only to lose 21 the next year.

Three young pitchers—Bob Friend, Vernon Law, and ElRoy Face—made their debuts in the early '50s. Each would later join the ranks of major league All-Stars.

The signing of shortstop Dick Groat turned out to be one of Rickey's better moves. Groat, a Wilkinsburg, Pennsylvania, native and a former basketball All-American from Duke, would later develop into a team leader and a National League MVP.

Joining Groat were other former college athletes. Twin brothers Johnny and Eddie O'Brien, who were featured in national headlines as basketball standouts for the University of Seattle, were selected as infielders. Vic Janowicz, a former All-American football player and Heisman Trophy winner from Ohio State, was named a catcher/third baseman.

"We could beat any other team in basketball or football," remembered catcher Joe Garagiola. "Unfortunately, we couldn't win baseball games."

He was right, of course. In 1951 the Bucs ended in seventh place, 32½ games out of first; in 1952 they posted a 42–112 record that landed them in the basement, 54½ games away from the pennant; in 1953 the team improved to a 50–104 record but still finished last, a full 55 games behind the league-leading Brooklyn Dodgers.

In a move that revealed his state of desperation, Rickey traded slugger Ralph Kiner to the Chicago Cubs on June 4, 1953. "It was the saddest day of my professional life," said Kiner. "The fans in Pittsburgh were always great to me."

With that one move Branch Rickey lost the support of most Pittsburghers. He had traded away their hometown hero. Even the most neophyte baseball fan now believed that decisions about the club were dictated by money. That should have been obvious

YOU BE THE JUDGE

The 1890 Pittsburgh Alleghenies posted a 23–113 record and ended the season 66½ games behind the first-place Brooklyn Superbas. The only player of national fame on this team was Billy Sunday, who would become a household name not because of his play in right field, but as one of the nation's most famous evangelists following his retirement from baseball. Since then no other ballclub representing the Steel City became the subject of more caustic remarks than did the 1952 Pirates.

Other modern-day clubs came close to matching the ineptness of the '52 Bucs. The 1941 Philadelphia Phillies (43–111), the debut season of the 1962 New York Mets (40–120), and the 2003 Detroit Tigers (43–119) are among the most notable. The '52 Pirates, however, would match any of these teams in terms of testing the patience of the manager, the media, and the fans.

Was this the worst team in Pirates history? You be the judge.

"In an eight-team league, we should've finished ninth," admitted catcher Joe Garagiola. Actually, that year the team fell only 55½ games behind another Brooklyn team—the Dodgers.

Slugger Ralph Kiner was the only player with the potential to deliver a "wow" factor. En route to leading the league for an amazing seventh consecutive year in home runs (37), he was the main reason people came to the ol' ballpark. Pitcher Murry Dickson, the workhorse of the mound staff, tossed nearly 278 innings and a respectable 3.57 ERA but finished with a league-leading 21 defeats. The remainder of the team, for the most part, seemed to be stuck in neutral.

Perhaps we can best put the accomplishments (or lack thereof) of this infamous squad in perspective when we see how they ranked among the existing eight teams in the National League.

Category	League Avg.	Team	Ranking
ERA	3.73	4.65	Last
Saves	18.3	8	Last
Shutouts	11.3	4	Last
Strikeouts Registered	655	564	Last

Category	League Avg.	Team	Ranking
Base on Balls Allowed	518	615	Last
Complete Games	55.5	43	Last
Runs Per Game	4.17	3.32	Last
Fielding Average	.977	.970	Last
Errors	143	182	Last
Batting Average	.253	.231	Last
Doubles	209	181	Last
Triples	42.3	30	Last
Home Runs	113.4	92	Last
Slugging Average	.374	.331	Last
Stolen Bases	49.5	43	Fifth*

*The team leader in stolen bases that year (9) was Brandy Davis. The fleet-footed center fielder, however, batted only .179. Ralph Kiner once observed, "If baseball allowed players to steal first base, Brandy would be in the Hall of Fame."

the year before when Rickey elected to field an array of only 21 players (four short of the number on any other team) on road trips to save a few dollars.

"In an eight-team league, we should've finished ninth," said Garagiola, a catcher for Rickey's teams for a bit longer than two years. Garagiola would later earn fame not for his baseball prowess, but for his quick wit as a radio and television broadcaster.

Manager Billy Meyer grew increasingly frustrated with a team that obviously lacked the talent to compete in the National League. One day, following a loss to Cincinnati in which the Bucs blew a four-run lead in the ninth inning, Meyer screamed at his players in the locker room: "You clowns could go on *What's My Line?* in full uniforms and still stump the panel."

Replacing Meyer in 1953 with congenial manager Fred Haney did little to improve the Pirates' fortunes. In Rickey's six seasons as general manager from 1950 to 1955, the Bucs, in an eight-team league, finished in seventh place one time and last five times.

Haney was gone as manager after three years. He later stated that his hands were tied during his tenure because Rickey had

BY THE NUMBERS

2—Pirates pitchers who have won the Cy Young Award (Vernon Law, 1960, and Doug Drabek, 1990)

ordered him to play youngsters and develop talent in lieu of winning ballgames.

When he turned 75 Rickey realized that he had lost the magical touch that had enabled him to mold Brooklyn into a perennial World Series contender. Following the 1955 season, he resigned as Pirates general manager and accepted a much less demanding role as a vice president.

Thus ended the saga of what had become known around Major League Baseball as the Rickey Dinks—still described by baseball aficionados as one of the worst periods for any big-league team.

One positive dimension grew out of this generation of "trial and terror" authored by Branch Rickey. The Mahatma, as some called him, did possess the insight to discover some players with raw talent who would surpass the predictions of other scouts and so-called experts. At times he fought not only other owners but also some of his Pirates colleagues to get their signatures on Pirates contracts. Among Rickey's signings were two pretty fair country ballplayers named Mazeroski and Clemente.

IN THE CLUTCH

The most highly prized moments in Pirates history for any fan is when a player or a team comes through in key situations with an unforgettable play that snatches a victory from the grasp of defeat.

The following are a few of these cherished moments in the history of the Pittsburgh Pirates—a club that has earned a reputation for doing precisely the right thing at the right time.

THE 1909 WORLD SERIES

The spanking-new ballpark known as Forbes Field was just three months old when the Pittsburgh Pirates finished the 1909 season with 110 wins and only 42 losses, six and a half games ahead of the fabled Tinker-to-Evers-to-Chance Chicago Cubs. It was the most wins ever for the Pirates, and the fifth highest in major league history. What makes this achievement even more amazing is the fact that the team compiled 110 victories when clubs played only 154 games during a regular season.

Pirates owner Barney Dreyfuss had spent considerable money in providing the people of Pittsburgh with the world's finest baseball park, as well as with a crop of players that knew how to win.

For the most part, the Pirates infield was average in terms of offense. At first base was Bill Abstein (.260, one home run).

Arguably the greatest shortstop in major league history was "the Flying Dutchman," Carnegie's own Honus Wagner, who was instrumental in winning the 1909 World Series for the Bucs.

Holding down second base was Jack "Dots" Miller (.279, three home runs). William "Jap" Barbeau guarded the hot corner at third, although he was the weakest link in the infield—hitting only .220 and committing 29 errors before he was dealt in August to the Cardinals for Bobby Byrne.

The one everyday player who could be considered a team standout was a native of nearby Carnegie, Pennsylvania, who covered shortstop and was arguably the greatest ever to play the position. John Peter "Honus" Wagner racked up enough hits that year to be awarded, for the fourth-straight season, the trophy for the senior circuit's batting champion (.339). The Flying Dutchman also led the league in doubles (39), RBIs (100), and slugging average (.489). Although not enough to lead in stolen bases, his 35 swipes testified to the fact that, at age 35, he could still run with the best of them.

Pittsburgh's outfield included Owen "Chief" Wilson (.272, four home runs), Tommy Leach (.261, six home runs), and Fred Clarke (.287, three home runs). Behind the plate was catcher George Gibson (.265, two home runs).

The figures reveal that this version of the Pirates was not over-loaded with home-run power. The mighty Wagner hit just five, and the entire team managed to hit only 25.

Pitching was the primary factor for the Bucs' success that year. Veterans Samuel "Howie" Camnitz (25–6, 1.62 ERA), Vic Willis (22–11, 2.24 ERA), Albert "Lefty" Leifeld (19–8, 2.37 ERA), and Charles "Deacon" Phillippe (8–3, 2.32 ERA), consistently tamed the opposition. The talented staff was joined by a new kid on the block, now in his first full year in the majors—Charles "Babe" Adams (12–3, 1.11 ERA). What team today wouldn't envy those low earned-run averages?

The Pirates' impressive record in 1909 was no fluke. Coming off a second-place finish the year before—only one game behind the Chicago Cubs, who would go on to win their last World Series that year—player/manager Fred Clarke demonstrated his ability to get the most out of the talent given him.

Awaiting the Pirates for the World Series were the Detroit Tigers, who had just won their third-consecutive league championship. To

PITTSBURGH'S BABE

One of the more pleasant surprises of the Pirates' pitching staff in 1909 was the addition of a 5'11", 185-pound right-hander from Tipton, Indiana, named Charles Benjamin "Babe" Adams.

Adams previously had two brief stints in the majors. The first came in 1906 with the St. Louis Cardinals when he posted a record of 0–1 and a whopping 13.50 ERA. The second was one year later with the Pirates, for whom he pitched a grand total of 22 innings and allowed 40 hits, ending the season with a mark of 0–2 and an improved, albeit hardly inspiring, 6.95 ERA.

Starting in 1909, however, something strange happened. In the 130 innings he pitched, Adams allowed not one batter to hit a home run, and he compiled a 12–3 record with an eye-popping 1.11 ERA. In addition, Adams set a record by pitching three complete games in a seven-game World Series against the Detroit Tigers, winning each one of them.

The naïve 27-year-old Adams created good copy for sportswriters in Pittsburgh and other National League cities, yet few of them knew his real first name. Because his youthful appearance made him look so young among the sea of veterans on the club, the rookie was christened "Babe." Following Adams's impressive showing in the World Series, player/manager Fred Clarke called him his "baby on the spot."

Adams would continue to pitch for the Pirates for 16 more seasons and win 194 games.

the journalists at newspapers throughout the nation, however, this was not so much a battle between two winning baseball teams. Instead, the 1909 World Series was a stage for a duel between the two superstars of Major League Baseball—the Pirates' Honus Wagner and the most famous (or infamous) player ever to don the uniform of the Detroit Tigers, Tyrus Raymond "Ty" Cobb.

Cobb, known as the Georgia Peach, had already established himself as the most feared competitor on a baseball diamond. Cobb did whatever it took to win a baseball game. To him, anyone wearing an opposing uniform was his enemy. Before or after a game, Cobb could be civil to that player; he might even have dinner with him following the game. Once the first pitch was tossed, however, he was an antagonist.

One of the most famous photographs from the era shows Cobb sliding into third base, cleats high, aiming for the legs of a helpless third baseman awaiting a throw from the outfield.

In addition to his roughhouse tactics, Cobb possessed such superior skills in the fundamentals of the game, it's little wonder he was among the first five Hall of Fame inductees 27 years later. He led the American League with a .377 average and 76 stolen bases. He also topped the junior circuit in runs scored (116), RBIs (107), hits (216), and, for the only time in his brilliant career, home runs (9).

Joining Cobb in the lineup for Detroit were "Wahoo" Sam Crawford (another future Cooperstown honoree), who led the junior circuit in doubles (35) and hit a respectable .314, and shortstop Owen "Donie" Bush, who batted .273. Pitcher George Mullin led the American League with 29 wins and only eight losses. Also having remarkable seasons were hurlers Ed Summers (19–9) and Ed Willett (21–10). Old reliable Wild Bill Donovan had, for him, an off year (8–7).

In Game 1, Tommy Leach brought Forbes Field's overflow crowd of more than 29,000 to its feet when he made a spectacular leaping catch of Cobb's towering fly ball in the seventh inning with two on and two outs to preserve a 4–1 victory for young Babe Adams and the Pirates.

HOW COLD WAS IT?

At the start of one of the World Series games between Pittsburgh and Detroit in 1909, invited to throw out the ceremonial first pitch of the game in the Motor City was Dr. Frederick A. Cook, the first man to explore the frigid North Pole just a year earlier. According to veteran Tigers broadcaster Ernie Harwell, Cook remained in the stands for only three innings before he had to leave. His excuse: "It was too cold for comfort."

Detroit won Game 2 by a score of 7–2 when the Tigers overcame a 2–0 Pirates lead and racked up nine hits off pitchers Camnitz and Willis. A steal of home by Cobb in the third inning sealed Pittsburgh's fate, and Detroit's Bill Donovan went the distance, limiting the Bucs to five hits.

Before a comparatively small crowd (18,277) at Bennett Park in Detroit, Nick Maddox of the Pirates held off a late Tigers rally, pitching all nine innings for an 8–6 win in Game 3. Honus Wagner was the hitting star with three singles, two RBIs, and three stolen bases.

Detroit's George Mullin posted 10 strikeouts in Game 4, as Pirates hurlers Lefty Leifeld and Deacon Phillippe could do

Pitcher Charles "Babe" Adams earned his nickname because of his youthful countenance.

IT'S A GREAT STORY

Baseball overflows with legendary stories that reveal the character of players. One of the more famous tales involves the two archrivals in the 1909 World Series.

Honus Wagner had gotten most of the headlines in the National League by winning his fifth-consecutive batting title. The American League's best player was Ty Cobb, who also led his league in hitting that year.

Cobb, never at a loss for finding ways to intimidate opposing players, hit a single to center to start the first inning of Game 1 of the Series in Pittsburgh. While taking sizable leads off first, Cobb taunted Wagner: "Hey, Krauthead. I'm coming down on the next pitch."

As soon as Pirates pitcher Babe Adams released the ball, Cobb took off for second. The barrel-chested Wagner, with blacksmith-like arms, covered the bag and grabbed catcher George Gibson's throw. Cobb slid, spikes high. The burly, 6', 200-pound Wagner sidestepped the onrushing Tiger, then swung his gloved hand across Cobb's jaw with a vengeance. The blow from Wagner's glove cut Cobb's lip and loosened two of his teeth. Umpire Francis "Silk" O'Loughlin bellowed: "Yer out!"

It was payback time.

For years, this was a favorite story often repeated around Pittsburgh taverns and other gathering spots for sports fans. There's only one thing wrong with the story. It's completely unfounded. Newspaper reports of Game 1 reference only one attempted steal of second by Cobb, and he made it.

But, as they say in baseball circles, it makes for a good story.

---

nothing more than watch in frustration as the Bucs were white-washed 5–0.

Back in the Steel City, Pittsburgh gained a 3–2 lead in the Series in Game 5 as Babe Adams returned to pitch nine solid innings in an 8–4 victory. Fred Clarke led the way with a three-run homer in the seventh that broke a 3–3 deadlock.

A strange schedule put the Series back in Detroit for Game 6, a game that was marred by injuries to three Detroit players. While chasing a bunt, first baseman Tom Jones ran over Pirates base runner Chief Wilson and was knocked unconscious. Charles "Boss" Schmidt and George Moriarty were both spiked while attempting to tag Pirates base runners. In spite of this, George Mullin bested Pittsburgh's Willis, Camnitz, and Phillippe 5–4 to deadlock the Series three games apiece.

Again in Detroit for the deciding Game 7, Babe Adams returned to the mound for his third appearance in the fall classic. With only two days' rest, he proved to be more than up to the challenge as he blanked the Tigers on six hits. Clarke walked four times in the game, while Wagner and Dots Miller each had two RBIs to give the Pirates eight runs—more than enough to send the Bucs home to pop champagne corks as winners of the World Series.

What about the hyped battle between the giants (Wagner and Cobb) in the 1909 World Series? It was really no contest. Wagner batted a healthy .333 during the seven-game Series; Cobb hit a mediocre .231. Wagner had six stolen bases; Cobb only two.

As a bonus, the 18 stolen bases by the Pirates tied a Series record.

Statistics aside, of primary importance to Pittsburgh fans were two undeniable facts. First, they had a new teen idol in town—Babe Adams—who was named the MVP of the Series. Second, their beloved Pirates, for the first time in their history, were the champions of Major League Baseball.

THE 1925 WORLD SERIES

Pirates owner Barney Dreyfuss never shied away from controversy. To the contrary, one of the secrets of his success lay in the fact that he was willing to take a risk if he sincerely believed he was in the right. That attitude prevailed whether he was investing millions of dollars in the construction of a first-rate baseball park or sacrificing a few players—even good ones—if he thought it would improve the Pirates.

Prior to the 1925 season, Pittsburgh had gone 16 years without appearing in a World Series. Sometimes during that span the Bucs came close. Just the year before, for example, they finished in third place, just three games behind the pennant-winning New York Giants. Neither Dreyfuss nor the Pittsburgh fans, however, were content to be "also-rans." They coveted the day when they could be called "champions."

At the annual owners' meeting in October, Dreyfuss took yet another bold move. He traded three of the Pirates' most popular stars—Charlie Grimm, Walter "Rabbit" Maranville, and Wilbur Cooper. In exchange, Pittsburgh received from the Chicago Cubs infielder George Grantham, rookie first baseman Al Niehaus, and pitcher Vic Aldridge.

Reporters at the *Pittsburgh Chronicle-Telegraph* were less than optimistic about the trade. Maranville and Grimm, especially, had been fan favorites. Their impish style brought additional life to the games with on-the-field pranks, such as the time Maranville, while stealing second base, dove headfirst between the legs of umpire Hank O'Day. Cooper was a solid pitcher, winning 20 games the previous season and 23 a year earlier.

The players received in exchange were dull by comparison. Aldridge had shown promise as a starting right-hander with Chicago over the past five years, but he was only a .500 pitcher. Grantham batted .316 the previous year and hit 12 home runs, but he was an erratic infielder who was tagged with the unflattering nickname "Boots" as a commentary on his defensive skills. He also led the league in strikeouts (63). Outside of his immediate family, nobody had ever heard of Niehaus.

Pirates manager Bill McKechnie was optimistic as the club began its season. He was asked to guide the youngest team in Major League Baseball, but he knew each player would give his best efforts every game.

That optimism seemed to be mere fantasy as the Pirates fell to last place on May 9. In addition, that unknown acquisition from the Cubs—Niehaus—was batting a woeful .212 and was sent to ride the bench.

For some unexplained reason, the team made an abrupt about-face and began to show promise. With timely hitting, strong pitching, and daring base running, the Pirates inched their way up the ladder and challenged for first place. Established stars such as Pie Traynor (.320, six home runs), the former Lutheran Seminarian Max Carey (.343, five home runs), Kiki Cuyler (.357, 18 home runs), Clyde Barnhart (.325, four home runs), and Glenn Wright (.308, 18 home runs) eventually showed the hitting skills for which they had become famous. Newcomer George Grantham (.326, eight home runs) not only hit for average but also showed vast improvement in the field at first base and cut his total strikeouts down to 29.

Sometimes the potency of the hitting attack surprised even the Pirates. In back-to-back games, the Bucs scored 21 runs against the Brooklyn Dodgers and 24 against the St. Louis Cardinals. Carey hit for the cycle in the first of these two, while Cuyler slammed two home runs, a single, and a triple.

Speed was an oft-used weapon of the Pirates. Finishing first and second in steals in the National League were Carey (46) and Cuyler (41). In one game Carey stole second, third, and home.

Pitching for the Bucs was an improved Vic Aldridge (15–7, 3.63 ERA), along with Pirates ace Lee Meadows (19–10, 3.67 ERA), who had 20 complete games, Ray Kremer (17–8, 3.69 ERA), Johnny Morrison (17–14, 3.88 ERA), and Emil Yde (17–9, 4.13 ERA). Babe Adams, the only leftover from the 1909 world champions, was now an "old man" at age 34 and relegated mostly to a mop-up role.

The Pirates picked up two more key players and a respected coach during the season. John "Stuffy" McInnis, a 17-year veteran recently released by the Red Sox, hit .368 in 59 games for the Bucs. The other was pitcher Tom Sheehan, who was acquired in a trade for the disappointing Niehaus.

A familiar name brought on board became a pioneer for Major League Baseball. Former manager Fred Clarke, who had guided the Pirates to their last World Series in 1909, was called out of retirement from his ranch in Kansas by owner Dreyfuss to serve as a "bench coach"—a position never designated by any club before— to assist Manager McKechnie. Perhaps it was just coincidence, but when the new coach took his seat in the dugout next to McKechnie, the Pirates began their serious drive for the 1925 pennant.

A MAJOR LEAGUE WRITTEN REPRIMAND

The celebration in the Pirates' clubhouse following the 9–7 victory in Game 7 of the 1925 World Series matched the euphoria of screaming children seeing their presents on Christmas morning. Players leaped high, shouted, hugged, and poured Iron City Beer over the heads of their teammates. A weeping Barney Dreyfuss, in a rare display of emotion, hugged William McKechnie and shouted, "You did it, Bill! You did it!"

Some of the exuberant players volunteered tales about how they were going to spend the $5,332 winners' checks each would receive the next day.

This carnival setting was in stark contrast to the gloomy atmosphere in the locker room of the defeated Washington Senators. The young player/manager Bucky Harris tried to keep a stiff upper lip and encourage his men to prepare for next year.

Harris's attempt to instill confidence in his team, however, was nearly derailed within minutes. American League president Ban Johnson was livid over the fact that Harris failed to lift Walter Johnson, who had obviously run out of gas. With the anger of a jilted lover, the president dashed off a pointed telegram to Harris that read: "You sacrificed a world championship for our league to mawkish sentiment."

Ouch!

By the end of the campaign, the Buccos surpassed even the wildest dreams of management and fans when they captured the crown by eight and a half games over the Giants.

The Steel City was aglow with excitement as the Bucs prepared to battle the talented Washington Senators. Led by one of the greatest pitchers of all time—Walter "Big Train" Johnson—the Senators were the reigning world champions. The future Hall of Famer had dominated the league, leading all other pitchers in victories for six of his 21 seasons and in strikeouts for 12 of them. He ended his career with an astounding record of 417–229. Now in his 19th season, he still had enough left in him to post a 20–7 mark.

Washington had other future inductees into baseball's shrine at Cooperstown. Leon "Goose" Goslin, the team's leading home-run hitter with 18, led the American League in triples with 20. Outfielder Sam Rice hit .350 with 227 hits. Shortstop Roger Peckinpaugh was second to none in fielding his position; that fact coupled with his respectable .294 average earned for him that year's MVP award for the American League. Player/manager Stanley "Bucky" Harris hit a respectable .287 while setting the standard for fielding at the keystone sack. His contemporaries also spoke of him as one of the best at motivating players.

On both offense and defense, the two teams seemed evenly matched. Where Washington may have had an advantage was on the mound. Besides the 37-year-old Johnson, southpaw Walter "Dutch" Ruether, in his first year with the Senators following a trade, was 18–7, and Stanley Coveleski, known for his spitball (a pitch that's since been banned), led the league with a 2.84 ERA and posted an impressive 20–5 record.

Johnson faced Lee Meadows in Game 1 at Forbes Field on October 7. Aided by a home run from the bat of Washington's Joe Harris, the Big Train limited the Pirates to five hits. The only reason for the more than 41,000 partisan fans to cheer came when they watched Pie Traynor slam a home run in the fifth inning. With the final score 4–1, the Senators showed why they had won two consecutive league championships.

The next afternoon, Vic Aldridge squared off against Stan Coveleski in a classic pitchers' duel. Senators first baseman Joe Judge made Pittsburgh fans think that this would be a repeat of Game 1 when he blasted a home run into the right-field stands in the second inning. Glenn Wright made the fans feel much better when he hit one into Schenley Park in the bottom of the fourth. The score remained tied at 1 when, in the home half of the eighth, shortstop Peckinpaugh uncharacteristically booted a ground ball for an error. The next batter, Kiki Cuyler, hit a 2–0 pitch from Coveleski and sent it over the wall. With the Bucs ahead 3–1, Washington made it close with a sacrifice fly in the ninth, but Aldridge registered two quick outs to preserve the 3–2 win.

The Series moved to Washington for Game 3. Ray Kremer started for Pittsburgh; Washington countered with Alex Ferguson. The Pirates scored first on a triple by Traynor and a sacrifice fly in the top of the second. Washington tied it with a single by Rice and a double by Judge in the third.

In the fourth, a double by Cuyler and a single by Barnhart gave the Pirates a 2–1 lead. They made it 3–1 in the sixth on a run-scoring hit by Kremer.

A Goose Goslin homer in the sixth and some timely hitting one inning later resulted in three runs for the Senators.

With his team leading 4–3 in the eighth, Senators reliever Frederick "Firpo" Marberry quickly disposed of the first two batters he faced on strikeouts. Pirates catcher Earl Smith then smacked a drive to deep center field. Outfielder Rice raced back toward some temporary bleachers constructed for the Series at Griffith Stadium. Rice dove into the crowd and emerged, holding high his glove showing the ball. The umpire ruled it an out. Pirates manager McKechnie protested loudly, saying that the umpire could not have seen if Rice had actually caught the ball and was able to keep it in his glove. It proved to be wasted lung power; as is most often the case, arguments with the umpire fell on deaf ears, and the Pirates' inning was over.

In the ninth, it looked as though the Bucs might pull it out when, after one out, Pirates infielder Eddie Moore singled, as did Carey. When Cuyler was hit by a pitch, the bases were loaded. Marberry, however, retired Barnhart on a pop-up and got Traynor to fly out to save the 4–3 victory.

Walter Johnson again showed why he was one of the best of all time when he shut out the Pirates 4–0 in Game 4. Supported by a Goslin home run and some sparkling defensive play by player/manager Bucky Harris, the Senators flexed their muscles, knocked Pirates starter Emil Yde out of the box in the third inning, and ended the day with a 3–1 edge in the Series.

With their backs to the wall, Pittsburgh vowed to come out fighting. McKechnie called on Aldridge to keep the Pirates in the Series. The manager's choice did not look good when Washington scored a run on Goslin's double.

WHERE CAN WE PUT 'EM ALL?

Imagine, for a moment, that you are hosting a dinner party at your home. You have everything set for the six guests who have informed you that they'll be in attendance. Suddenly, just two days before the scheduled event, you discover that at least 20 plan to show up.

Multiply that number by 2,000, and you'll understand Barney Dreyfuss's anxiety after his team won the National League pennant and was required to host the American League champion Washington Senators in Game 1 of the World Series at Forbes Field on October 7, 1925.

Beautiful Forbes Field was deemed by many as the finest ballpark in all of Major League Baseball. Its spacious outfield and majestic stands were unmatched in splendor.

Forbes Field, even with its newly added double-deck grandstand in right field, unfortunately, could seat barely 35,000 fans. With the onrush of requests for World Series tickets, especially from loyal fans in western Pennsylvania, West Virginia, and Ohio, Dreyfuss wanted to disappoint nobody; also, every additional patron who passed through the turnstiles generated additional profit.

The office secretary threw up her arms in frustration. "Where can we put 'em all?" she asked.

Dreyfuss donned his thinking cap to devise ways in which he could squeeze as many bodies as possible in the stands and remain within the existing fire codes.

First, he added extra seats in front of the regular stands along the foul lines. Second, he crammed as many fans as possible in the aisles and in passageways behind the grandstands. Finally, in that spacious distance of 110 feet between home plate and the screen (sometimes dubbed the "catcher's outfield"), Dreyfuss created a special "press section" for newspaper reporters who had traveled to the Steel City from throughout the nation.

The sea of fans and journalists seated in these extra seats sometimes hindered the view of the catcher, but Dreyfuss was able to pack more than 43,000 people into the park for Game 2 and Game 6.

In spite of these rather spartan conditions, none of the fans voiced a complaint to Dreyfuss or to any executive in the Pirates front office. Everyone was just happy to be there.

Washington's starter Coveleski looked tired but was able to subdue the Pirates until the top of the third when Carey singled and stole second. Carey broke his rib sliding into the base but insisted on remaining in the game. A walk to Cuyler, a single by Barnhart, and a sacrifice fly by Traynor gave the Bucs a 2–1 lead.

Joe Harris tied the game with a home run in the fourth, but the Pirates went ahead 4–2 in the seventh as a result of a walk to Moore and singles by Carey, Cuyler, and Barnhart.

Rice's run-scoring single brought the Senators within one run in the bottom of the inning.

The Pirates breathed a bit easier when Wright doubled and McInnis singled him home for one run in the eighth, and Wright singled home another insurance run in the top of the ninth.

The 6–3 lead was everything Aldridge needed; he quietly set the Senators down in the bottom of the ninth.

Back in Pittsburgh, with the Senators holding a 3–2 game edge, hopes dimmed for Pirates fans as Washington scored a run in both the first and second innings off starter Ray Kremer. Pie Traynor's single in the bottom of the third tied the contest and brought a rousing cheer from the 43,810 fans, who squeezed the last bit of standing room out of Forbes Field.

Eddie Moore, the only Pirates starter who failed to hit .300 during the regular season, showed why he belonged with his talented teammates when he belted a home run in the fifth to put the Pirates ahead 3–2.

When Kremer shut down the Senators the rest of the way, he and the Pirates tied the Series at three games apiece.

In sports, there are few moments as exciting as the seventh game of a World Series. Following seven months of preparation (counting spring training), two baseball clubs and their fans look to this game as the one thing that can make or break an entire season.

With no tomorrow, both managers pulled out all stops. Washington manager Harris summoned his ace Walter Johnson once again. Could this aging icon reach deep inside himself for yet another victory? Vic Aldridge took the hill for the Pirates with only two days' rest.

The weather suddenly became front-page news. On this rather chilly October 15, the skies opened and rain cascaded on all of Allegheny County.

Not wanting to lose the revenue from the packed house at Forbes Field, and because rain was forecast for the next few days, Dreyfuss opted to play the game.

The skies appeared to grow even darker when Washington scored four big runs in the top half of the first. After yielding two hits, three walks, and two wild pitches, a disappointed Aldridge turned over the ball to reliever Johnny Morrison after getting only one out.

Meanwhile, Sir Walter kept the Pirates in check until the third. Morrison's single, Moore's double, Carey's single, and Barnhart's single, all off an obviously tiring Johnson, narrowed the gap to 4–3.

Washington picked up two more runs in the top of the fourth, due in part to Max Carey slipping and falling on the mud-soaked field, as the fans sat silently while wet and shivering in their seats.

The Bucs got back a run in the home half of the fifth when both Carey and Cuyler doubled.

Ray Kremer, now on the mound for Pittsburgh, kept the Senators' bats quiet over the next two innings. In the bottom of the seventh, with the skies becoming even darker, the Pirates tied the game as Moore hit a pop fly to short that the normally sure-handed Roger Peckinpaugh dropped for his seventh error in the Series. Carey sent a screaming double down the left-field line that Washington unsuccessfully argued was actually foul, and Moore crossed the plate. Traynor then lashed a triple to left-center field, scoring Carey, and was called out at the plate trying to stretch it into a home run.

Peckinpaugh atoned for his error when he smacked a home run in the top of the eighth, putting the Senators ahead by a run.

A very tired Johnson returned to the pitching rubber, now surrounded by sawdust in an attempt to keep the surface dry. As the rains fell harder, Smith doubled and pinch-hitter Carson Bigbee lined another two-bagger to tie the score at 7.

To the amazement of nearly everyone watching the game, Manager Harris refused to remove his ace pitcher, whose arm was as limp as the drenched uniforms of the players. Moore walked. Carey hit a slow grounder to short, but Pekinpaugh's throw to second was high and late. All runners were safe. With the bases loaded, Cuyler earned his salary for the year when he drove one of Johnson's pitches to left center for a double, scoring two runs.

The rain throughout the afternoon progressed from sprinkles to a drizzle to a steady downpour. But the fans seemed oblivious to this when the Pirates took the field for the ninth inning.

Manager McKechnie called on pitcher John "Red" Oldham, a midseason recruit from the minors who had not pitched in the big leagues for three years, to protect the 9–7 lead. The 32-year-old struck out Rice, got Harris to line out to Moore at second, and, with three sharp-breaking straight curve balls, struck out Goose Goslin to end the game and the Series.

The Pirates were world champions for the second time in their history. As the 42,856 jubilant fans, who had endured the horrible weather that afternoon, left Forbes Field, most of them didn't notice that for the first time all day the sun was beginning to shine.

THE 1971 WORLD SERIES

"If you get me to the postseason, I'll put you on my back and carry you to the Promised Land."

That bold promise was delivered to his teammates during a players-only meeting during the second half of the 1971 race for the National League pennant by the only man who could make that statement. He was Roberto Clemente, known in baseball circles as the Great One.

Clemente may not have won any oratorical contests during his lifetime, but few speakers could have been more persuasive. After all, he knew what it took to overcome adversity.

Born and raised in Puerto Rico, Roberto Clemente Walker (his full name) faced a double dose of prejudice when he joined the Pirates in 1955. Not only was he linked with African Americans, but he was also a product of the Latino community—something rarely seen in Major League Baseball at that time.

In Pittsburgh support for Clemente was limited at best. His erratic mood swings sometimes resulted in his sitting out games while physically healthy. That did nothing to endear him to the work-a-day world of Pittsburgh fans.

Gradually Clemente gained respect from the fans and his fellow players. His skills as a hitter that earned him four National League batting titles, his daring running on the base paths, his ability to hit for power, and his cannonlike arm generated a brand of excitement never before seen on a Pirates ball field. By 1971, he was the undeniable leader in the clubhouse and the sports hero of the city.

The Pirates seemed to have a virtual lock on first place for most of the season, but going into September their lead had dwindled to only four and a half games. Clemente's speech helped them to refocus on winning.

Instrumental in their assault on the opposition were some key players. The 37-year-old Clemente finished fourth in the race for the batting title with a .341 average plus 13 home runs and 86 runs knocked in. He also won his 11th consecutive Gold Glove award. Outstanding performances that year were also given by outfielder Willie Stargell (.295, 48 HR, 125 RBI), catcher Manny Sanguillen (.319, 7 HR, 81 RBI), second baseman Dave Cash (.289, 2 HR, 34 RBI), outfielder Al Oliver (.282, 14 HR, 64 RBI), and first baseman Bob Robertson (.271, 26 HR, 72 RBI).

Statistics might indicate that Bucs hitters showed much more power at the plate this season. But this was the first full year in which they played at the new Three Rivers Stadium—a much friendlier venue for home runs than was spacious Forbes Field.

Leading pitchers for the Bucs that year were Dock Ellis (19–9, 3.06 ERA), Steve Blass (15–8, 2.85 ERA), Bob Moose (11–7, 4.11 ERA), and newcomer Nellie Briles (8–4, 3.04 ERA). Reliever Dave Giusti racked up 30 saves and was voted Fireman of the Year in the National League.

The Bucs would go on to win the Eastern Division pennant, besting the Cardinals by seven games.

Postseason records were not favorable to the Pirates. Just the previous year, the Bucs lost three straight games to Cincinnati in the National League Championship Series. And they had not participated in the World Series since Bill Mazeroski catapulted the historic blast into Schenley Park 11 years before.

The 1971 NLCS opened on October 2 in San Francisco. The Giants took the first of this best-of-five series by a score of 5–4, highlighted by a long home run by Willie McCovey off Pirates

GET ME TO THE CHURCH ON TIME

Pirate Bruce Kison had a lot of things on his mind during the month of October 1971. First, he was a 21-year-old rookie in the major leagues. Second, he was a member of the National League champions who were playing the Baltimore Orioles in the World Series. Third, he was unexpectedly called on to pitch in a critical situation in the first inning of Game 4 when Baltimore had already scored three runs. Fourth, he was on cloud nine after tossing a stunning 6⅓ innings of shutout ball and credited with a Series win. And, oh yes, he was scheduled to get married in Pittsburgh immediately following Game 7.

Unfortunately, Game 7 was played in Baltimore.

As soon as the Orioles' Merv Rettenmund grounded out to end the final game, giving the Bucs a 2–1 victory, the young Kison had no time to join his teammates in popping corks in the locker room. Instead, he and his best man, Bob Moose, quickly showered, then hurried to a waiting helicopter sitting in the parking lot of Memorial Stadium that whisked them away to a private jet at the airport.

In a miracle finish that was second only to the Pirates' triumph earlier that afternoon, the bridegroom and his best man arrived at the church only 20 minutes late.

Years later, the media and fans learned that the last-minute details were arranged and paid for by Bucs broadcaster Bob Prince.

Why did Kison not know that the final game of the 1971 World Series would be held in Baltimore?

Call it a rookie mistake.

starter Steve Blass. Since Pittsburgh had dropped five of the six games they played in Candlestick Park that year, this came as no surprise. But the Bucs rebounded with a 9–4 win with solid pitching from Dock Ellis and three home runs by Robertson and one from outfielder Gene Clines.

Back in Pittsburgh, the Pirates kept the winning spirit alive with a 2–1 victory behind the five-hit pitching of Bob Johnson and home runs by Robertson, who would be named the Series MVP, and Richie Hebner.

In the final game, Pittsburgh flexed its muscles with a convincing 9–5 win at Three Rivers Stadium. Hebner hit a four-bagger, and Oliver, who was unhappy with being platooned in center field, took his anger out on a baseball that he smacked over the fence. Pitcher Bruce Kison picked up the win.

Now it was on to Baltimore and the World Series.

One of the great mysteries for Pittsburgh fans of this era was that few people outside of the Steel City considered Roberto Clemente to be a superstar. Perhaps it was because he played in a relatively small market that the exciting right fielder was not given his due.

The '71 World Series would change all that.

The Baltimore Orioles, under the baton of manager Earl Weaver, were perennial champions. Winning 101 games during the regular season—the third year in a row in which the club had at least 100 wins—and overpowering the Oakland Athletics three games to none in the American League Championship Series, the Birds from Baltimore were 5–3 favorites to take the fall classic.

The starting lineup had Hall of Fame candidates Brooks Robinson and Frank Robinson, plus four 20-game winners: Jim Palmer, Dave McNally, Pat Dobson, and Mike Cuellar.

Playing Game 1 at Memorial Stadium in Baltimore, the Pirates looked as if they wished to embarrass those Las Vegas oddsmakers by posting a three-run lead in the second inning due, in part, to some sloppy fielding by Baltimore's normally polished infield. Pitcher McNally, however, yielded just two hits the rest of the way, and the A's pecked away at starter Dock Ellis to notch a 5-3 win.

Things got no better in Game 2. Brooks Robinson showed why he has to be considered one of the greatest third basemen this side of Pie Traynor, with miracle stops of sharp ground balls. Baltimore went on to shell six Pirates pitchers with 14 hits in a humiliating 11–3 victory, dwarfing a three-run shot by Richie Hebner.

To many sportswriters around the country, the Series was over. Obviously, they claimed, Pittsburgh was no match for the American League champions. Even respected columnist Jim Murray of the *Los Angeles Times* caustically wrote that the Pirates might choose to be blindfolded before their pending "execution."

Game 3 in Three Rivers Stadium proved them all wrong. Blass, in one of his more masterful outings, limited the hot bats of Baltimore to only three hits with his pinpoint control. Catcher Manny Sanguillen stated that he could actually divide home plate into fifths, and Blass would hit the target each time.

With the Pirates leading 2–1 in the home half of the seventh and two runners on base, Murtaugh gave slugger Bob Robertson the sign to bunt. Robertson failed to see the sign. He swung at the first pitch, sending it high and deep into the left-field stands for a three-run homer.

The final score of 5–1 sent the 50,403 fans home with much more hope.

Game 4 will always be remembered as the first World Series game played at night. A record crowd of 51,378 packed the stands, while more than 61 million viewers throughout the country watched this prime-time telecast.

Murtaugh selected Luke Walker, a 10–8 pitcher, to start the game. Partisan fans scratched their heads at this choice, especially when the Orioles knocked the southpaw out of the box with three runs before the first inning was over. Saving the day for the Pirates was 21-year-old rookie Bruce Kison. The 6'4" right-hander,

BY THE NUMBERS

3—Most home runs ever hit by a Pirate during one game (done 16 times)

although showing signs of wildness, controlled the Baltimore hitters over the next 6⅓ innings on just one hit.

The Buccos came back with two runs in the bottom of the first and could have had two more in the third. With Hebner on base, Clemente smacked a deep fly down the right-field line. At that time, Three Rivers Stadium did not have traditional foul poles, making it more difficult for umpire John Rice to determine if the ball left the park fair or foul. He ruled the ball was foul. After vigorously protesting, the Great One returned to the batter's box and lined a single. Oliver then singled home Hebner with the tying run. Pirates pinch-hitter Milt May gained his 15 minutes of fame in the seventh when he hit a single, sending the tie-breaking run across the plate. That ended the scoring as Pittsburgh evened the Series at two games apiece.

Nellie Briles pitched the game of his life the next day when he blanked the Orioles on two hits. Aided by Bob Robertson's home run, the Pirates posted a 4–0 win to put them ahead three games to two.

Back in Baltimore for Game 6, Clemente hit a home run and a triple. It was not enough, however, as the Orioles, in 10 innings, bested the Pirates 3–2 with the winning run coming off a sacrifice fly by Brooks Robinson.

On October 17 for the crucial Game 7, Murtaugh called on Steve Blass to bring home the trophy. Mixing his 92 mph fastball with a slow curve he dubbed the "slop drop," Blass kept sluggers Boog Powell, Merv Rettenmund, and Frank Robinson off stride. Clemente hit his second home run of the Series, which proved to be the margin of difference as Pittsburgh won the final contest 2–1.

BY THE NUMBERS

5—Number of world championships won by the Pirates (1909, 1925, 1960, 1971, 1979)

The city of Pittsburgh rolled out the red carpet for their World Series champions. During a parade through the downtown streets, the fans saved their loudest screams for the three heroes of the Series.

Murtaugh helped win the Series through some daring moves and player selections. He also was masterful in working with some temperamental men who could have tested the patience of a saint. Shortly after the music from the parade's marching bands faded and the city's cleanup crews swept away the last bits of confetti from Smithfield Street, the beloved manager announced that he would not return the next season—making this the third time he would "retire" from the game.

Blass worked two complete games, allowed only seven hits, registered 13 strikeouts, and compiled a 1.00 ERA. "I was numb for two days afterward," he confessed.

Clemente, with an amazing .414 average, two homers, and dazzling defense in right field, was named the Series MVP.

For the first time, the entire nation learned what Pittsburgh fans had known for a number of years: Clemente was in a class all by himself.

FIRST IN WAR

Pitcher Hugh Mulcahy, who was part of the mound staff during the 1947 season, will never be linked with the all-time great right-handers in Major League Baseball, but he will be forever enshrined in America's Hall of Fame.

Mulcahy, a 6'2", 190-pound native of Brighton, Massachusetts, started his career with some bad Philadelphia Phillies teams prior to World War II. In a recent edition of *The Black and Gold*, the Pirates alumni newsletter, Pittsburgh writer David Finoli described Mulcahy as one of the most underestimated hurlers in the history of baseball.

"Despite the fact he was a fine pitcher, his career mark was only 45–89. His .336 winning percentage is one of the worst of all time for pitchers with 100 or more decisions," he wrote. "Make no mistake, though, he was a heck of a pitcher with a tremendous fastball. In 1940, Mulcahy was selected to play in his one and only All-Star Game.

"A year later, losing games for the Phillies would become a distant memory. On March 8, 1941, Hugh Mulcahy became the first major leaguer to be drafted into the Armed Forces during World War II.

"While stationed in New Guinea, Mulcahy contracted dysentery, losing 35 pounds. When he returned in 1945 after giving up four years of his career in the service, Hugh lost the zip in his fastball because of the illness, causing him to be a shell of himself. He went 3–7 in two years in Philadelphia before ending his career with the Pirates in 1947.

"Never losing his sense of humor, Mulcahy quipped, 'Maybe I should have developed a knuckleball.'"

Following his year with the Bucs, Mulcahy settled in Beaver Valley where he devoted much of his time to charitable works prior to his death in 2001.

FOR THE GOOD OF THE COUNTRY

In his recent book *For the Good of the Country*, author Dave Finoli compiled a list of Pirates players who served in World War II:

Cal Abrams	Johnny Berardino	Bill Clemensen
Bob Addis	Jimmy Bloodworth	Dick Cole
Ed Albosta	Eddie Bockman	Dick Conger
Alf Anderson	Hank Borowy	Walker Cooper
Jim Bagby	Bobby Bragan	Billy Cox
Ed Bahr	Bill Brandt	Bud Culloton
Bill Baker	Jimmy Brown	Dutch Dietz
Vic Barnhart	Mace Brown	Bob Dillinger
Dick Bartell	Smoky Burgess	Erv Dusak
Monty Basgall	Max Butcher	Aubrey Epps
Russ Bauers	Hank Camelli	Ed Fernandes
Ted Beard	Jack Cassini	Les Fleming
Hank Behrman	Pete Castiglione	Elbie Fletcher
Fern Bell	Bob Chesnes	George Freese

In the Clutch

Larry French
Ken Gables
Huck Geary
Al Gionfriddo
Sid Gordon
Hank Gornicki
Earl Grace
Hank Greenberg
Ben Guintini
Harry Gumbert
Bob Hall
Jack Hallett
Wally Hebert
Ken Heintzelman
Rollie Hemsley
Billy Herman
Gene Hermanski
Johnny Hetki
Kirby Higbe
Jim Hopper
Lee Howard
Dixie Howell
Roy Jarvis
Wally Judnich
Red Juelich
Ken Jungels
Frank Kalin
Ralph Kiner
Bob Klinger
Clem Koshorek
Bob Kuzava
Clem Labine
Johnny Lanning
Paul LaPalme
Cookie Lavagetto
Ed Leip
Johnny Lindell

Johnny Logan
Vic Lombardi
Al Lyons
Jack Maguire
Woody Main
Stu Martin
Gene Mauch
Windy McCall
Moose McCormick
Clyde McCullough
Cal McLish
Jack Merson
Al Monchak
Walt Moryn
Ray Mueller
Joe Muir
Hugh Mulcahy
Red Munger
Danny Murtaugh
Steve Nagy
Rocky Nelson
Red Nonnenkamp
Fritz Ostermueller
Eddie Pellagrini
Jim Pendleton
Jack Phillips
Ray Poat
Johnny Podgajny
Howie Pollet
Bob Porterfield
Mel Queen
Marv Rackley
Pete Reiser
Dino Restelli
Rocky Rhawn
Hal Rice
Marv Rickert

Culley Rikard
Johnny Rizzo
Bill Rodgers
Stan Rojek
Tom Saffell
Jack Salveson
Hank Schenz
Bob Schultz
Vinnie Smith
Glenn Spencer
Bud Stewart
George Strickland
Jim Suchecki
Billy Sullivan
Max Surkont
Oad Swigart
Al Tate
Lou Tost
Virgil Trucks
Earl Turner
Maurice Van Robays
Ben Wade
Harry Walker
Junior Walsh
Bill Werle
Max West
Wally Westlake
Burgess Whitehead
Lefty Wilkie
Grady Wilson
Gene Woodling
Glenn Wright
Johnny Wyrostek
Eddie Yount
Frankie Zak

NUMBERS DON'T LIE
[OR DO THEY?]

An ancient adage goes something like this: "There are lies, damn lies, and statistics." That may apply to every phase of life except one—baseball.

One of the amazing things about America's pastime is that it depends not on how big or how strong a person might be. That person has every opportunity to excel in a sport that depends not on the luck of the draw, but on a person's skill at hitting a curveball or outrunning a ball that was destined to become an extra-base hit.

Another eye-popping truth about baseball is this: A hitter who is successful three times out of 10 is a candidate for the Hall of Fame. Another who is successful only two times out of 10 is headed for obscurity.

Numbers are more essential in baseball than in any other sport. Seldom, if ever, will any fan of football or basketball cite the statistics of a player. During any baseball game, however, it's common to hear people around you contrast what former icons have done as compared to modern-day players.

Within the Pirates family are players who have racked up impressive statistics. Some you may have already known; others may surprise you.

PIRATES PITCHING GREATS

The Pittsburgh Pirates have had some terrific hurlers on their staffs. Throughout their careers while wearing a Pirates uniform, here are some of the leaders.

Best ERAs
(1,000 Innings Pitched)

1. Vic Willis   2.08
2. Lefty Leifield   2.38
3. Sam Leever   2.47
4. Deacon Phillippe 2.50
5. Howie Camnitz   2.63
6. Kent Tekulve   2.68
7. Jesse Tannehill   2.73
8. Babe Adams   2.74 *t*
   Wilbur Cooper   2.74 *t*
10. Doug Drabek   3.02

Most Wins

1. Wilbur Cooper   202
2. Sam Leever   194 *t*
   Babe Adams   194 *t*
4. Bob Friend   191
5. Deacon Phillippe 168
6. Vernon Law   162
7. Rip Sewell   143 *t*
   Ray Kremer   143 *t*
9. John Candelaria   124
10. Bob Veale   116 *t*
    Jesse Tannehill 116 *t*
    Howie Camnitz   116 *t*

Strikeouts

1. Bob Friend   1,682
2. Bob Veale   1,652
3. Wilbur Cooper   1,191
4. John Candelaria   1,159
5. Vernon Law   1,092
6. Babe Adams   1,036
7. Steve Blass   896
8. Dock Ellis   869
9. Deacon Phillippe   861
10. Rick Rhoden   852

Pitcher Bob Friend led the Bucs in many categories during some lean years in the 1950s.

Best Winning Percentages
(100 Decisions)
1. Jesse Tannehill .667
2. Sam Leever .660
3. Vic Willis .659
4. Jack Chesbro .648
5. Deacon Phillippe .646
6. Lee Meadows .629
7. Ray Kremer .627
8. Al McBean .602
9. Doug Drabek .597
10. Rip Sewell .596

Saves
1. ElRoy Face 188
2. Kent Tekulve 158
3. Mike Williams 140
4. Dave Giusti 133
5. Jose Mesa 70
6. Stan Belinda 61
7. Al McBean 59
8. Bill Landrum 56
9. Jim Gott 50
10. Rich Loiselle 49

Shutouts
1. Babe Adams 44
2. Sam Leever 39
3. Bob Friend 35
4. Wilbur Cooper 33
5. Lefty Leifeld 29
6. Vernon Law 28
7. Deacon Phillippe 25
8. Vic Willis 23
9. Rip Sewell 20 *t*
   Bob Veale 20 *t*

Innings Pitched
1. Bob Friend   3,480.1
2. Wilbur Cooper   3,199
3. Babe Adams   2,991.1
4. Vernon Law   2,672
5. Sam Leever   2,660.2
6. Deacon Phillippe 2,286
7. Rip Sewell   2,108.2
8. Ray Kremer   1,954.2
9. John Candelaria   1,873
10. Bob Veale   1,868.2

Complete Games
1. Wilbur Cooper   263
2. Sam Leever   241
3. Deacon Phillippe 209
4. Babe Adams   206
5. Pud Galvin   167
6. Frank Killen   163
7. Bob Friend   161
8. Jesse Tannehill   148
9. Rip Sewell   137
10. Ray Kremer   134

Most Losses
1. Bob Friend   218
2. Wilbur Cooper   159
3. Vernon Law   147
4. Babe Adams   139
5. Sam Leever   100
6. Rip Sewell   97
7. ElRoy Face   93
8. Deacon Phillippe 92
9. Bob Veale   91 t
   Ron Kline   91 t

Home Runs Allowed

1. Bob Friend   273
2. Vernon Law   268
3. John Candelaria   172
4. ElRoy Face   130
5. Steve Blass   128
6. Ron Kline   124
7. Ray Kremer   122 *t*
   Murry Dickson   122 *t*
9. Rip Sewell   114
10. Doug Drabek   112

PIRATES HOME-RUN LEADERS

The Pirates have had more than their share of players who have led the National League in batting average. Home-run leaders were not that plentiful. Much of the reason was the immense size of the early home fields of the Bucs—Exposition Park and Forbes Field.

In spite of this, two Buccos, especially, left their legacies as being among the great sluggers of the game.

The following led or tied for National League home-run titles during their tenures with Pittsburgh:

Year	Player	Total
1902	Tommy Leach	6
1946	Ralph Kiner	23
1947	Ralph Kiner	51
1948	Ralph Kiner	40
1949	Ralph Kiner	54
1950	Ralph Kiner	47
1951	Ralph Kiner	42
1952	Ralph Kiner	37
1971	Willie Stargell	48
1973	Willie Stargell	44

THEY LED THE LEAGUE IN HITTING

If it is true that the single most difficult challenge in all of sports is to hit a round ball, with a round bat, tossed by a major league pitcher, then the Pirates have had more than their share of players who have demonstrated that this can be done with amazing frequency.

The following is a list of the Bucs who have led the National League in batting average:

Year	Player	Average
1900	Honus Wagner	.381
1902	Ginger Beaumont	.357
1903	Honus Wagner	.355
1904	Honus Wagner	.349
1906	Honus Wagner	.339
1907	Honus Wagner	.350
1908	Honus Wagner	.354
1909	Honus Wagner	.339
1911	Honus Wagner	.334
1927	Paul Waner	.380
1934	Paul Waner	.362
1935	Arky Vaughan	.385
1936	Paul Waner	.373
1940	Debs Garms	.355
1960	Dick Groat	.325
1961	Roberto Clemente	.351
1964	Roberto Clemente	.339
1965	Roberto Clemente	.329
1966	Matty Alou	.342
1967	Roberto Clemente	.357
1977	Dave Parker	.338
1978	Dave Parker	.334
1981	Bill Madlock	.341
1983	Bill Madlock	.323
2006	Freddy Sanchez	.344

Swinging some powerful bats during the late 1950s were Pirates sluggers (left to right) Dick Stuart, Dale Long, and Frank Thomas.

RBI LEADERS

Baseball legend Lou Gehrig coined the slogan "The most important statistic for a hitter is not home runs, but in the number of runs he bats in."

Six Pirates over the years have led the National League in this vital category:

Year	Player	Total
1901	Honus Wagner	126
1902	Honus Wagner	91
1906	Jim Nealon	83
1908	Honus Wagner	109
1909	Honus Wagner	100
1911	Owen Wilson	107
1912	Honus Wagner	102
1927	Paul Waner	131
1949	Ralph Kiner	127
1973	Willie Stargell	119

PIRATES POWER

The Pittsburgh Pirates have seldom led the National League in home runs, primarily because, during their first 83 seasons, they played in ballparks—Exposition Park and Forbes Field—that required gargantuan swats in order to clear the walls. At the same time, the Pirates have had their share of home-run sluggers who have left fans gasping upon seeing the towering blasts.

Some of the big hits by players wearing a Pirates uniform are:

1907: Honus Wagner hit the longest ball ever recorded at old Exposition Park when he slammed one high over the head of the Philadelphia center fielder Roy Thomas to the deepest part of the park. Due to a charley horse, aggravated when first baseman Kid Gleason purposefully bumped Wagner, who had just reached first base, Wagner was able only to hobble into third.

1950: Ralph Kiner grabbed the attention of big-city media when he powered long drives at the Polo Grounds in New York and Braves Field in Boston. In Pittsburgh, local fans who saw a drive off Cincinnati hurler Kent Peterson will remember a clout that cleared the 25-foot scoreboard in left field by at least 50 feet and was still rising when it exited Forbes Field. Writer Les Biederman of *The Pittsburgh Press* described it as "the longest and hardest ball that ever flew off his mighty bat. The crowd gasped as the ball started for home-run territory, and so did Peterson."

1959: Roberto Clemente is not known primarily as a power hitter, but on May 17, he hit one that Chicago fans still discuss with awe. In deep center at Wrigley Field is a giant scoreboard that rests 500 feet from home plate. No batter has yet to hit that familiar sight, but Clemente came closest when he poked one that sailed out of the ballpark just to the left of the scoreboard. In attendance that day was Hall of Famer Rogers Hornsby, who testified that Clemente's ball was the longest he had seen hit in 45 years of baseball.

1959: Dick Stuart was the first to ignore the fact that the batting cage was always moved to the deepest part of left-center field, because, everyone believed, nobody could ever hit a ball that far during a game. On June 5, he tagged Cubs pitcher Glen Hobbie for a 500-plus-foot orbit over the cage and the wall. Stuart's modest reaction was, "It was one of my best shots, but I can't really say if it was my very best."

1964: Clemente, again, showed an amazing display of power when, at Forbes Field, he crushed a fastball off the Dodgers' Sandy Koufax that bounced 30 feet high off a light tower in center field on May 31.

1966: In Forbes Field on June 5 and June 9, Clemente clubbed balls over the 435-foot sign in right-center field, off Houston's Turk Farrell and Cardinals pitcher Al Jackson, respectively. "I didn't think anyone could hit a ball that far," said St. Louis outfielder Curt Flood.

1969: Willie Stargell celebrated Independence Day when, on July 4, he hit one of his seven home runs over the roof at Forbes Field, this one off future Hall of Famer Tom Seaver. Stargell later said it was "the best I ever hit."

1969: On August 5, Stargell became the first player ever to hit a ball completely out of Dodger Stadium in Los Angeles—a 480-foot smash. He repeated the feat several times, including a 512-foot bomb that is still considered the longest ball ever hit in that venue.

THE FAM-A-LEE

I f there was ever a time when the great city of Pittsburgh was united, it was during the exciting baseball season of 1979. During this era, the highest paid CEO of a corporation shared "high fives" with a homeless person pushing a grocery cart along Fort Duquesne Boulevard.

Headline makers that year were not about world leaders or national politicians. Instead, they were local heroes named Stargell, Foli, Candelaria, Tekulve, and Tanner.

The 1979 World Series, as it turned out, would be a microcosm of baseball and of life. Down three games to one, the underdog Pittsburgh Pirates rallied to overcome otherwise impossible odds by defeating the Baltimore Orioles. In the midst of their remarkable comeback was the tragic death of the manager's mother.

Perhaps no other team in Major League Baseball has ever responded to the challenge as the '79 Bucs did. It is in this spirit that you are invited, once again, to celebrate the year of the Fam-A-Lee.

THE MAGNIFICENT 1979 PITTSBURGH PIRATES

The year is 1979. America is in a funk.

Double-digit inflation, a near disaster at Three Mile Island, the capture of 52 Americans in Iran, and the decline of downtown businesses placed over the city of Pittsburgh a cloud that grew

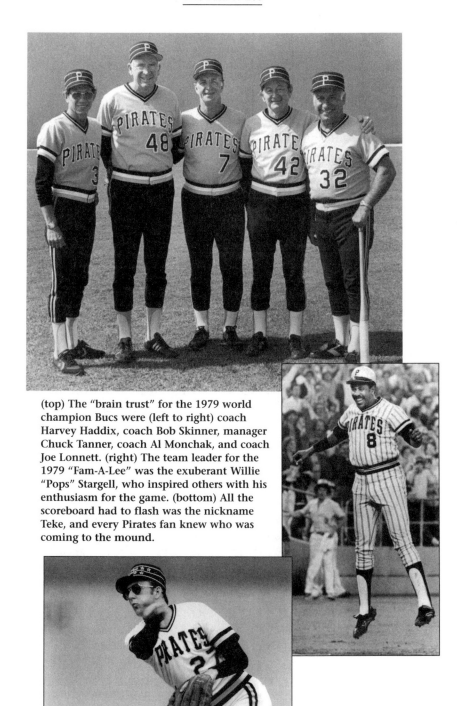

(top) The "brain trust" for the 1979 world champion Bucs were (left to right) coach Harvey Haddix, coach Bob Skinner, manager Chuck Tanner, coach Al Monchak, and coach Joe Lonnett. (right) The team leader for the 1979 "Fam-A-Lee" was the exuberant Willie "Pops" Stargell, who inspired others with his enthusiasm for the game. (bottom) All the scoreboard had to flash was the nickname Teke, and every Pirates fan knew who was coming to the mound.

darker than the smoke that rose from the Homestead Works 25 years earlier.

Into this atmosphere of doom and gloom came a cause to celebrate. The 1979 Pirates, under the baton of manager Chuck Tanner, included a cast of characters known as Scrap Iron, Cobra, Teke, the Candy Man, and, of course, Pops.

The team became a cardiologist's nightmare as the Bucs compiled a 98–64 regular-season record, winning 25 of the games in their last at-bats.

But that wasn't the whole story. They had something else. They had an impossible mission, a dynamic leader, and an unforgettable song.

That, in a nutshell, is the story of the 1979 Pittsburgh Pirates.

The year before, they came so very close to winning it all, finishing in second place just one and a half games behind Philadelphia in spite of a late-season surge fueled by timely hitting by outfielder Dave Parker. This year, they vowed, they would not be cheated.

Showing their determination, general manager Harding "Pete" Peterson signed Parker, considered by many as the game's most complete player of the time, to a five-year, $7 million

NOW, *THAT'S* CONFIDENCE

What made the '79 version of the Pittsburgh Pirates so special? Kent Tekulve, the Pirates' ace reliever, may have had the answer. There were two things, according to the one known as Teke—attitude and confidence.

As far as attitude, "It was a team that was unselfish and did not care about who the hero was from top to bottom," he said.

He also spoke about a confidence that bordered on cockiness.

"We used to sit on the bench and we'd be down by a couple of runs in the sixth or seventh inning. We'd look over to the other team and start laughing at them. We'd say, 'Look at them; they think they're winning. They don't know we've already got three runs we haven't scored yet.'

"We knew we were going to come back," he said.

contract. Following a failed attempt to land Cincinnati's perennial All-Star Pete Rose (who chose to join the Phillies), Peterson managed to acquire pitcher Enrique Romo from Seattle, the feisty shortstop Tim Foli from the New York Mets, the young, hard-hitting Mike Easler from the Red Sox organization, and, from San Francisco, southpaw pitcher Dave Roberts.

The roster, now complete, gave Tanner enough offense and defense to leave no doubt that the Pirates would be a contender.

As happens so very often with Pittsburgh teams, the 1979 squad did not get a fast start out of the gate. By Memorial Day, the Bucs were six and a half games behind the Montreal Expos and Philadelphia Phillies.

Adding to the concern of Tanner was the fact that the man who had been the Pirates' superstar for the past decade—Willie Stargell—had turned 39 years old before Opening Day.

In late June Peterson brought in the former two-time batting champion Bill Madlock from the Giants. As it turned out, he was the key that unlocked the door to success.

Stargell, the patriarch of the team, got new life. Now in his 18th season with the Bucs, Stargell became the team counselor, the teacher, the motivator, and the overall leader.

After a particular player did something noteworthy on the field, Pops, as the players affectionately called him, handed that player a felt star that could be worn on his hat. These "Stargell Stars" were esteemed badges of honor proudly worn by players. Stargell was no clinical psychologist, but creating and distributing those stars became one of the better motivational techniques of all time.

There was one other factor. It came neither from the Pirates front office nor from any player on the field. It came, instead, from across the state—North Philadelphia, to be specific. A quartet (later a trio) known as Sister Sledge recorded a disco hit song titled "We Are Family." During a rain delay, as Stargell and his teammates were sitting in the dugout waiting for the weather to clear, over the loudspeakers came the sounds of the recording. The players started to sing along. It had that certain "feel" that added some sunshine to the gloomy afternoon.

During the final game at Three Rivers Stadium in 2000, the group Sister Sledge, along with the Pirate Parrot, lead the Pirates faithful in singing "We Are Family."

Stargell picked up the telephone in the dugout and called the press box. He told them to announce to the crowd that this was now the Pirates' official clubhouse song.

Everything now seemed to work. Prior to the All-Star break, the Pirates won six of their last seven games. Although they were still mired in fourth place, they were only four games out of first.

The Family, as they were now called, inched their way toward the top and by season's end finished in first place, two games ahead of Montreal.

By now, all of Pittsburgh joined in the chorus of "We Are Family." The song was the most often played recording on radio. Fans held hands in the stands and danced with complete strangers while singing the words.

Facing a tough Cincinnati squad with stars such as Joe Morgan, Johnny Bench, George Foster, and Ray Knight, the Bucs won the best-of-five National League Championship Series, three games to none.

The singing increased in volume. Our Pirates were in the World Series.

Facing the Bucs were the awesome Baltimore Orioles. Led by future Hall of Fame pitcher Jim Palmer and slugger Eddie Murray, the O's were odds-on favorites to dominate the Pirates.

Game 1 of the Series made the betting experts look good as Baltimore took the first contest, 5–4, on a misty, 40-degree night at Memorial Stadium.

The Bucs rebounded the next night by squeaking out a 3–2 victory highlighted by a brilliant slide by catcher Ed Ott to score the tie-breaking run in the top of the ninth and some clutch relief pitching by Kent Tekulve.

Back in Pittsburgh for Game 3, manager Earl Weaver and his Birds overcame a 3–0 lead by the Pirates and bested John "Candy Man" Candelaria and the Bucs by a score of 8–4.

Game 4 did not add any smiles to the faces of the packed house at Three Rivers Stadium. In spite of a double and a home run slammed by Willie Stargell, Baltimore gained a decisive three-game-to-one advantage by scoring six runs in the top half of the eighth to win the game 9–6.

Las Vegas bookmakers announced that the Pirates were 100–1 underdogs. Pittsburgh's hopes looked as bleak as the approaching gray skies of winter.

A pall hung over the Pirates' locker room on Sunday, October 14. Not only were the Bucs on the cusp of losing the World Series, but Chuck Tanner just received the telephone call that every son expects one day to receive but is never prepared for. His beloved mother, Anna, had died just a few minutes before.

BY THE NUMBERS

6—Number of home runs hit by the Bucs' Tommy Leach to lead the National League in 1902

Tanner insisted on staying at the helm. "My mother would have wanted me to do that," he said.

Along with the theme song "We Are Family" came another battle cry. "We can do it for Chuck's Mom," shouted pitcher Grant Jackson.

Behind the six-hit pitching of Jim Rooker and Bert Blyleven, the Pirates sent seven runners across the plate to win by a score of 7–1. Pirates faithful dared to think that it just might be possible

A LASTING MEMORY

As a fitting tribute to the team and to its unquenchable spirit, today along Pittsburgh's Federal Street in front of PNC Park stands a 12-foot statue of the late, great Willie Stargell. Before or after each home game at PNC Park, many of those who were there during that '79 season pause near the base of that bronze replica of the powerful Pirates captain. They look with admiration at the bat held high and the imposing stare of the burly slugger peering out at a nervous pitcher who would rather have been waiting in a dentist's chair for a root canal without benefit of Novocain. The more observant point to the statue's lower hand, only three fingers of which grasp the bat. They all remember how the popular slugger twirled his bat like a windmill as he waited for the pitch. Their minds overflow with a legion of priceless memories of those smooth, potent swings and of the gargantuan homers that often followed. Most of all, they reflect on that wonderful, magical season.

In the eyes of most is a glimmer of hope that says: "Perhaps…just perhaps…in my lifetime, I can see another championship flag fly over this ballpark."

When they leave the statue and mentally reenter the real world of business and obligations, there's a renewed bounce to their steps. Some can be heard whistling, even singing, the refrain to "We Are Family."

And, why not? To them, this music is not merely an anthem of personal pride. It's a classic reminder of why baseball is the greatest game ever.

We Are Fam-A-Lee!

May that song never end.

BY THE NUMBERS

7—Number of consecutive years Ralph Kiner led or tied for the National League lead in home runs

for the Fam-A-Lee to overcome insurmountable odds and prove to the city, and to themselves, that miracles still occur.

Could they win the remaining two games over Baltimore in its home park? John Candelaria and Kent Tekulve thought they could when they blanked the O's, 4–0, to knot the Series at three games apiece.

When Stargell hit a two-run homer in the top half of the sixth over the outstretched glove of outfielder Ken Singleton to put the Pirates ahead, 2–1, every player on the team felt a quiet confidence that it was only a matter of time. With the addition of two more runs (one resulting from a hit batsman with the bases loaded) in the top of the ninth, the fat lady was about to sing.

Tekulve struck out the first two Baltimore batters in the home half of the inning and got pinch-hitter Pat Kelly to loft a game-ending fly ball to Omar Moreno. The cry went out all over Pittsburgh: "Our Fam-A-Lee has just won its fifth World Series in franchise history."

It was a glorious combination of a Series, a leader, a song, and a team no Pirates fan will ever forget.

HALLOWED GROUND

The oak wood of a stage at the original Grand Ole Opry, the black dirt and gray clay of the battlefield at Gettysburg, and a row of crimson bricks embedded in the grounds of the University of Pittsburgh all have something in common. They are sites of important happenings in America.

None of these landmarks is in perfect condition. Ryman Auditorium bears scuff marks from boots worn by Del Reeves, Johnny Cash, and Ernie Ford; the soil of Seminary Ridge and Cemetery Ridge at Gettysburg is mixed with the blood of troops commanded by Robert E. Lee and George Meade; the bricks of old Forbes Field are worn from the pacing of Pirates fans who, once again, attempt to relive the glorious memories generated by the likes of Kiner, Clemente, Mazeroski, and Stargell.

These settings, therefore, become more than mere points on a map. They are, in fact, hallowed grounds for Americans.

Baseball fans in Pittsburgh throughout the centuries have held special feelings for the sites at which they have cheered for their Pirates. Like other historic settings, not all were perfect. Recreation Park was subject to floods. Forbes Field's infield could be dangerous when attempting to field ground balls. Three Rivers Stadium was sterile. PNC Park, however, is a sign that someone finally got it right.

Good or bad, each of these venues has been a setting for the kind of adoration that approaches worship.

Just because these houses of thrills may have been built of wood, steel, or concrete, and featured, at times, synthetic playing surfaces, does not mean they lack souls.

RECREATION PARK (1887-1890)

Recreation Park was the first official home of the National League Pittsburgh Alleghenies, the name used by the team during its earliest years.

First Game—April 30, 1887, won by Pittsburgh, 6–2, against the Chicago White Stockings
Seating Capacity—17,000
Smallest Crowd—6 paid, 17 in attendance, April 23, 1890, vs. Cleveland Spiders

Although we know the ballpark was built on the North Side, next to the location where Three Rivers Stadium stood, its precise dimensions remain unknown. We do know that it was bordered by North Avenue on the north and the Pittsburgh, Fort Wayne, and Chicago Railroad tracks to the northeast, near Grant and Pennsylvania Avenues.

Probably the most bizarre happening at the park, aside from the team's inability to win games, involved Alleghenies catcher

HALLOWED GROUND

Every October 13, Pittsburgh fans gather at the portion of the Forbes Field center-field wall that remains in Oakland. They listen to a taped broadcast of Game 7 of the 1960 World Series. At 3:36 PM when they listen to the announcer exclaim "The ball..." they cheer and hug each other as if they were hearing if for the first time.

When asked why he and others make this annual pilgrimage to this site, longtime Pirates fan Todd Miller of Pittsburgh simply says, "Why not? After all, this is hallowed ground."

Fred Carroll's pet monkey that accompanied the team everywhere it went. The monkey died in 1887, and the team elected to bury their beloved pet with honors directly beneath home plate during a pregame ceremony.

EXPOSITION PARK (1891-1909)

Capacity—16,000
Dimensions
>Left Field—400 Feet
>Center Field—450 Feet
>Right Field—400 Feet

First Game—April 22, 1891, won by Chicago Cubs, 7–6
Final Game—June 29, 1909, won by Pittsburgh, 8–1, over the Chicago Cubs

Exposition Park was a huge field that yielded few out-of-the-park home runs.

Actually, this field could have been labeled "Exposition Park III," since two other venues were given this title prior to Pittsburgh joining the National League. Located where the east parking lot of Three Rivers Stadium used to sit, Exposition Park was the first field to host the team known as the Pirates.

Outside of attempting to hit a baseball over the deep outfield walls, the biggest challenge was keeping dry. Located near the banks of the occasionally overflowing Allegheny River, the park featured games that sometimes had to be played in ankle-deep water in the outfield. A special ground rule was invoked during those times: a batted ball hit into the flooded area was ruled a single.

To prevent the elements from dominating the playing surface more than necessary, the Pirates installed baseball's first roll-on tarp to protect the infield.

Games 4–7 of the first-ever World Series between Pittsburgh and the Boston Pilgrims in 1903 were hosted at Exposition Park. It was a festive time for the entire city, except for the fact that the Pirates lost three of those four games and eventually the Series.

A FIELD CALLED FORBES (1909-1970)

Cost of Construction—$1 million, including property acquisition
Seating Capacity—23,000 in 1909; 35,000 in 1925
Largest Crowd—44,932 vs. Brooklyn Dodgers, September 23, 1956
Smallest Crowd—200 on June 10, 1938, vs. the Philadelphia Phillies
Highest Season Attendance—1,705,828 in 1960
Lowest Season Attendance—139,620 in 1914
Dimensions:

Left-Field Foul Line: 360 feet (1909), 356.5 (1921), 356 (1922),
360 (1926), 365 (1930), 335 (1947), 365 (1954)

Left-Center Field: 462 feet (1909), 457 (1930)

Center Field: 442 feet (1926), 435 (1930)

Right-Center Field: 375 feet (1942)

Right-Field Foul Line: 336 feet (1909), 376.5 (1921), 376
(1922), 300 (1925)

Backstop: 110 feet (1909), 84 (1938), 80 (1947), 84 (1943), 75
(1959)

Barney Dreyfuss, owner of the Pittsburgh Pirates from 1900 to 1932, was a man ahead of his time. When he was a bookkeeper for the Louisville Colonels, he defied the skeptics by predicting that a winning baseball club would be a solid investment. He backed his prophecy by investing big dollars into obtaining quality ballplayers to form a first-rate club. As a result, his Pittsburgh franchise won three straight National League pennants from 1901 to 1903. The team eventually played in the first World Series between the National League

ALL-TIME HOME-RUN LEADERS AT FORBES FIELD

By Pirates:
Ralph Kiner—175
Roberto Clemente—85
Willie Stargell—74
Frank Thomas—64
Wally Westlake—62

By Visiting Players:
Eddie Mathews—38
Willie Mays—31
Hank Aaron—31
Gil Hodges—27
Del Ennis—26

and the upstart American League in '03. Before then baseball's postseason competitions were known by various other names, including the Championship of the United States and the Temple Cup.

Dreyfuss continued to enhance his reputation as a visionary when, in 1908, he announced his plan to construct a massive, two-tiered baseball park for the fans of Pittsburgh.

While most ballparks were made of wood, Dreyfuss noted that he would be more ambitious by constructing the new facility out of steel and concrete.

"When I told people about the new ballpark, they laughed," admitted Dreyfuss. "When I told them where I planned to build it,

During its first week of operation in 1909, Forbes Field drew Pittsburghers in their finest attire. Some arrived at the ballpark in horse-drawn carriages, while others sported the new high-tech mode of transportation called automobiles. (Photo obtained from the *Pittsburgh Post-Gazette* photo archives)

they laughed even harder. It was on property belonging to Schenley Farms, complete with livery stable while a few cows roamed over the countryside."

Some of the less optimistic members of the press dubbed the structure that was two miles east of downtown Pittsburgh "Old Ironsides." The most caustic scribes called it "Dreyfuss's Folly." Its real name was Forbes Field, in memory of a British general who captured Fort Duquesne from the French in 1758 and renamed it Fort Pitt in honor of Prime Minister William Pitt.

There's debate about exactly how much the structure cost Dreyfuss to build. According to official Pirates records, the total charged by the lead architect, Osborne Engineering, and the Nicole Construction Company was $1 million, including land acquisition. Other estimates show it cost nearly twice that amount. Whatever the final figure, it was, even in that era, a remarkable bang for the buck for a ballpark that would seat 25,000 people—more than could be seated at New York's Polo Grounds, which the Giants and Yankees would share for another 13 years.

SOME FORBES FIELD LASTS

June 29, 1970

Last Run Scored—Al Oliver (Pirates)
Last RBI—Bob Robertson (Pirates)
Last Home Run—Al Oliver (Pirates)
Last Hit—Willie Smith (Cubs)
Last Batter—Don Kessinger (Cubs)
Last Win—Jim Nelson (Pirates)
Last Save—Dave Giusti (Pirates)
Last Loss—Milt Pappas (Cubs)

"A friend of mine bet me a $150 suit of clothes that the park would never be filled," said Dreyfuss. "We filled it five times the first two weeks."

The first game at Forbes Field was on an ideal afternoon at 1:30 on June 30, 1909, before a standing-room-only crowd of 30,388. Pittsburgh Mayor William A. Magee tossed the ceremonial first pitch from Box 137, in the center of the upper deck, to John M. Morin, director of the Department of Public Safety. He took the ball to Pirates star pitcher George Gibson, who had taken his position on the mound.

"This is the happiest day of my life," exclaimed Dreyfuss.

CLEARING THE ROOF

On May 25, 1935, the legendary Babe Ruth, while playing in his last season with the Boston Braves, did something that nobody else had done previously at old Forbes Field. Among his three home runs that afternoon, the Babe launched his last career blast—number 714—over the 86-foot rightfield stands.

Since that day, the feat was duplicated 17 more times by eight other players.

Here is a list of those 18 monstrous shots:

1. Babe Ruth (Boston Braves)—May 25, 1935
2. Ted Beard (Pirates)—July 16, 1950
3. Mickey Mantle (New York Yankees)—April 10, 1953 (exhibition game)
4. Wally Moon (St. Louis Cardinals)—April 30, 1957
5. Bob Skinner (Pirates)—July 25, 1958
6. Eddie Mathews (Milwaukee Braves)—September 21, 1959
7. Eddie Mathews (Milwaukee Braves)—July 14, 1960
8. Bob Skinner (Pirates)—June 3, 1962
9. Jerry Lynch (Pirates)—August 12, 1964
10. Rusty Staub (Houston Astros)—June 4, 1966
11. Willie Stargell (Pirates)—July 9, 1967
12. Willie Stargell (Pirates)—August 18, 1967
13. Willie McCovey (San Francisco Giants)—June 23, 1968
14. Willie Stargell (Pirates)—July 4, 1969
15. Willie Stargell (Pirates)—August 16, 1969
16. Willie Stargell (Pirates)—August 26, 1969
17. Willie Stargell (Pirates)—April 20, 1970
18. Willie Stargell (Pirates)—April 25, 1970

Pirates manager Fred Clarke announced to the enthusiastic crowd, "Pittsburgh can now boast of the world's finest baseball park. It needs only one thing more. Instead of that flag inscribed 'Forbes Field,' it should have a banner inscribed, 'Pittsburgh, Champions of the World.' Sounds like a dream? So did Forbes Field, when Barney first thought of it. But it may come true."

The hometown faithful lustfully cheered their Bucs. Unfortunately, enthusiasm in the stands does not always equal victories, as Pittsburgh dropped its opener to the Chicago Cubs. Fans who attended the first game were astounded by the spaciousness of the new ballpark. A catcher had 110 feet between home plate and the backstop to catch a foul pop fly. The left-field wall was more than 360 feet away, and right field a bit farther. Center field was a pitcher's paradise, with red brick walls 462 feet away. It was so mammoth that the batting practice hitter's cage could be left against the inside wall during games.

Over the course of the next 61 years, Forbes Field's dimensions were altered to fit more Pirates fans into the ballpark.

With the addition of double-deck right-field stands, a tall screen varying between 14 and 18 feet compensated for the foul line that was shortened to 300 feet. This feature was to help prevent "cheap" home runs. During World War II, that screen could not be repaired or replaced aue to the need for steel in the war effort. It deteriorated badly from 1941 to 1945.

Following the signing of Detroit slugger Hank Greenberg to a contract prior to the 1947 season, Pirates management opted to reduce the left-field fence to 335 feet with the addition of an eight-foot fence, dubbed "Greenberg Gardens." The temporary structure, made of wood and chicken wire, stretched from the foul line to left-center field. The 30 feet between the front of the "Gardens" and the outside brick wall served as bullpens for both teams.

Forbes Field is still remembered by seasoned fans as an ideal place to watch a ballgame. Quite possibly, their memories are more than a little enhanced by time. The reality is that some spectators faced what we might call...ah...challenges. For example, some fans had to sit behind thick, steel posts that supported the roofs on both the first and second tiers. Depending on what was happening on the field, patrons unfortunate enough to sit here had to move from side to side in order to see the action.

If you wanted to have a totally unobstructed view at a reasonable price, you could join the nearly 2,000 partisans who sat in the bleachers along the left-field line.

The bleachers became a popular venue for anyone who wanted to watch the games for less than half the cost of a general admission ticket. One dollar was the highest price ever charged for a seat on one of these planks of wood, which had barely enough room for a thin posterior to be placed between two painted lines. The entertainment value, indeed, was a blessing for those who wanted to see a ballgame for next to nothing; however, there was a trade-off. Spectators had to sit facing the outfield; if they wished to see the action between pitcher and hitter, they had to keep their heads turned to the right. Following a Sunday doubleheader, many of these die-hard enthusiasts ended up with stiff necks that lasted until Tuesday. In addition, fans in the upper-left corner of the bleachers could not see home plate because the third-base grandstands blocked their view.

Watching a game at Forbes Field could offer other challenges, but they were mild compared to those playing on the field. An outfielder chasing after a hard-hit ball to left-center or right-center field had to contend with the base of light towers on the grass. Also, the aforementioned batting cage and a tall flagpole sat in left-center field; a ball hitting either of those fixtures was deemed "in play."

The infield introduced another heap of obstacles. Comprised of clay and red dirt, the extremely hard surface contained tiny pebbles that could cause a bad hop and turn the tide of any contest. Just ask Yankees shortstop Tony Kubek.

In the bottom of the eighth inning in the dramatic Game 7 of the 1960 World Series, the Pirates were trailing the Bronx Bombers, 7–4. With Gino Cimoli on first and one out, Bill Virdon hit a sharp ground ball to shortstop that looked like a tailor-made double play. Not so at Forbes Field. The ball hit one of those little stones, bounced straight up, and hit Kubek in the throat, knocking him to the ground and out of the game. Both runners were safe.

"Maybe God could have done something about that play; man could not," remembered Yankees manager Casey Stengel.

For all practical purposes, after all the construction was completed, Forbes Field seated around 35,000 spectators. Sometimes

KEEPING THE SABBATH HOLY

As an evangelist, few in American history were as influential as Billy Sunday. He was often photographed with mayors, governors, and even the president of the United States. Using an approach to preaching the gospel known as "hell-fire and brimstone," the popular Sunday was instrumental in establishing the period known as Prohibition in the United States.

Not only did Sunday oppose the selling of alcohol, but he also felt that engaging in any sort of recreation on the first day of the week was not the proper way to "keep the Sabbath holy." He, therefore, contacted every owner of a Major League Baseball club and reminded them of this commandment.

His influence obviously went beyond the pulpits and the sawdust trails in the canvas revival tents. Most of the clubs (including Pittsburgh) banned the playing of baseball on Sundays.

Even after the courts ruled in 1934 that playing baseball on Sunday was legal, the evangelist's influence prevailed. At Forbes Field, for example, as late as the mid-1950s no inning could be started after 7:00 PM on Sunday so that fans would still have time to attend evening vespers that normally began at 7:30.

during the days of extended winning streaks or popular promotions, the attendance swelled to more than 40,000. Not to miss out on an opportunity to take advantage of the increased size of the gate, Pirates management persuaded paying customers to sit four- and five-deep on the outfield grass in front of the right-field wall. The fans agreed to give way to outfielders attempting to catch a fly ball. If a batted ball rolled into the temporary seating area, a special rule awarded the batter a double.

Beer and baseball have been a traditional blend for more than a century. At Forbes Field, however, beer was not sold until the mid-1950s. Fans, nonetheless, could bring their own bottles of Duquesne Pilsner, Iron City, Fort Pitt, or Silver Top to the game as long as they maintained good conduct.

Forbes Field was the setting for many events that are memorable to Pittsburgh baseball fans. To list them all would fill a

BY THE NUMBERS

8—Number of times Honus Wagner led the National League in batting average (1900, 1903, 1904, 1906, 1907, 1908, 1909, 1911)

volume by itself. Nevertheless, older Pirates fans may recall one or more of these moments in time that they saw with their own eyes:

- Broadcaster Harold Arlin sitting in a box seat behind the first-base dugout speaking into a microphone as he becomes the first person ever to broadcast a baseball game. He did so over KDKA radio on August 5, 1921.
- An aging Babe Ruth shuffling slowly off the field following a single, concluding a spectacular afternoon of hitting that included his last three home runs—sending the final one, number 714—over the roof of the right-field stands, on May 25, 1935.
- Bowed heads of fans during the singing of the national anthem during the 1943 season as they faced a 32-foot-high, 15-foot-wide wooden statue of a United States Marine against the left field in honor of servicemen fighting in World War II.
- A humble and shy Dale Long being pushed out of the dugout by his teammates during a five-minute standing ovation on May 28, 1956, to make the first-ever "curtain call" in big-league history after he hit a home run in his eighth consecutive ballgame.
- Bill Mazeroski skipping around the bases, waving his cap over his head after hitting a ninth-inning home run on October 13, 1960, to win the World Series over the highly favored New York Yankees.
- Willie Stargell hitting any of his seven home runs over the 86-foot-high wall in right field.

Even with all of its foibles and lack of sophistication, Forbes Field was home to Pirates fans. On June 28, 1970, 40,918 squeezed into the aging ballpark. At the conclusion of a doubleheader with the Cubs (swept by the Bucs, 3–2 and 4–1), the fans stood and cheered as Mazeroski fielded a ground ball by Don Kessinger and stepped on second base to retire Willie Smith on a force-out. It would be the final out of the last game in Forbes Field. The fans who were there can testify that the enthusiastic applause was not so much because the Pirates won both games, but mostly in appreciation for all they had received from this grand old lady called "Forbes."

What ever happened to Forbes Field? The hallowed grounds of this historic ballpark were purchased by the University of Pittsburgh. The university leveled the field in 1971 and constructed new buildings for its campus.

As a gesture of goodwill to the many fans who remember the great times they spent there, the university left three reminders of the ol' ball yard:

1. A portion of the left-center-field red-brick wall, with the painted white number "457," marking the wall's distance from home plate. In front of the wall is the flagpole that was located on the playing field.
2. A metal plaque along a sidewalk marking the spot over which Mazeroski hit his Series-winning blast in 1960.
3. The last home plate used at Forbes Field, encased in glass in the lobby floor of the university's Posvar Hall. The location of the plate, however, is not exactly where home plate sat. Had architects placed home plate in its precise spot, about half of the Pirates fans could not view it. The reason: it would have to be on display in the fifth stall of the ladies' restroom.

BY THE NUMBERS

10—Number of consecutive games the Pirates won to start the 1962 season, giving rise to talk of a World Series championship. The team finished in fourth place, eight games off the pace.

THREE RIVERS STADIUM (1970–2000)

Cost of Construction—$35 million
Seating Capacity—48,044
Surface—Artificial Turf
Dimensions:
   Left-Field and Right-Field Foul Lines—340 feet (1970), 335 feet
      (1975)
   Left-Center Field and Right-Center Field—385 feet (1970), 375
      feet (1975)
   Center Field—410 feet (1970), 400 feet (1975)
   Outfield Walls—10 feet high
   Backstop—60 feet from home plate
First Game—July 16, 1970, lost by Pittsburgh to Cincinnati, 3–2
Final Game—October 1, 2000, lost by Pittsburgh to Chicago,
   10–9

Three Rivers Stadium, constructed on Pittsburgh's North Side
just east of PNC Park, was the result of current thinking that a
multipurpose stadium would help serve the 'Burgh's quest for a
modern facility that could provide a fitting venue for both baseball and football. It was a popular approach for sports arenas
during this time in other cities, such as Atlanta, Cincinnati,
Houston, St. Louis, and Philadelphia.

Designers of Three Rivers followed a logical course in their
development of the facility. With equal distances down the foul
lines, both right-handed and left-handed batters would face
similar challenges. Artificial turf would help ensure fair bounces.
A circular stadium would allow fans to view the games relatively
unobstructed in seats that were three inches wider than those at
Forbes Field. Private, high-dollar corporate boxes would provide
more revenue for team owners.

A state-of-the-art, 30' x 240' scoreboard high above the left-
center-field seats not only announced in bright, bold letters who
was at-bat, but also, through computerized cartoon characters and
graphics, urged the crowds to cheer.

Three Rivers Stadium had all that a fan would ever want,
except one thing—passion. Following a few years in which the

Steel City demonstrated an initial surge of excitement, aided by some fine ball teams in the early '70s, attendance quickly waned.

Fans complained that they had difficulty driving to and from the ballpark. The parking lots were slow to empty. Others were disappointed when they had to sit so high (the stadium had six levels of seats), that they felt too far away from the action.

The relatively poor showing of the club in the 1980s did not help in generating enthusiasm. Even when the Pirates were in the playoff games in the early '90s, the team could not fill the stadium.

Three Rivers produced great memories over the 30 years. They included nine Eastern Division titles, two National League pennants, and two World Series championships. Individual feats remain topics of conversation among the faithful: Roberto Clemente's 3,000th hit; no-hitters by the Bucs' John Candelaria in 1976 and a combined no-hitter by Francisco Cordova and Ricardo Rincon in 1997, won on a tenth-inning home run by Mark Smith; and bombastic upper-deck blasts by Willie Stargell that were memorialized by painted numbers on the seats where they landed.

The stadium began to show its age early. The need for repairs and possible reconstruction led Pirates owners to campaign for a new home park. Through a combination of political arm-twisting and energetic promotions, funds became available to construct a new, more baseball-friendly stadium. Plans were made to demolish the 8,000 tons of metal and concrete as soon as possible.

Sally O'Leary, a longtime, faithful member of the Pirates front office and editor of the Pirates' Alumni Association newsletter, *The Black and Gold*, wrote about the last day of the stadium that brought so many great memories to fans of the Bucs:

"It was a beautiful sunny morning, 21-degree temperatures, on Sunday, February 11, 2001. In just 19 seconds, [Three Rivers Stadium] became a pile of rubble and dust at 7:59 AM.

"More than 20,000 people viewed the blast and bid adieu to the stadium that had brought so many highs and lows in Pirates history since 1970.

"It was a festive atmosphere, with helicopters and blimps circling around, vendors selling T-shirts and fans throwing parties. Yet it was bittersweet in many ways, with so many memories of the great home runs, the championships, the no-hitters, the tough losses, and the close victories over the years.

"Those of us who spent a good deal of our lifetime at Three Rivers will always treasure the good days at the proud structure, and will carry our memories right along with us to our new ballpark, where we can compile a whole new list of things to remember and cherish.

"As our friend, Bob Prince, said many times, 'Kiss it, Goodbye.'"

PNC PARK (2001–PRESENT)
Cost of Construction—$216 million
Seating Capacity—38,496
Surface—Natural grass
Dimensions:
Left-Field Foul Line—325 feet
Left-Center Field (with a 410-foot nook dubbed the "North Side Notch" by announcer Steve Blass)
Center Field—399 feet
Right-Center Field—375 feet
Right-Field Foul Line—320 feet
Walls—The right-field wall rises 21 feet (in memory of the legendary Roberto Clemente, who wore uniform No. 21), drops down to 10 feet in center field, and drops again to just six feet in front of the left-field bleachers.
First Game—April 9, 2001, Cincinnati 8, Pittsburgh 2

"The more things change, the more they remain the same."
It's an old expression, and it was never more accurate than in describing the concept, design, and construction of the most beautiful ballpark in Major League Baseball—PNC Park.
The home of the Pittsburgh Pirates since 2001, PNC Park, so named when PNC Bank bought the naming rights, combines the

Who can argue with the claim that PNC Park is the most beautiful in all of baseball?

best features of old Forbes Field and the progressive spirit of the Steel City.

Anyone who attends a game in this magnificent structure is struck first by the panoramic view of the downtown skyline. Rising above the outfield walls are the Gulf Building and the Koppers Building, along with the modern PPG Place and Fifth Avenue Place, offering to each fan a mosaic of a proud history and of an exciting future for the Steel City.

The second impression is the closeness of the fans to the field. Unlike the antiseptic, aloof feeling yielded by its predecessor, PNC Park provides an intimacy akin to that offered by other classic sites such as Wrigley Field and Fenway Park, with the highest seat just 88 feet from the field.

In short, PNC Park is not a stadium. It's a ballpark.

Fans can get a taste of the festive atmosphere even before crossing the turnstiles. Prior to game time, anyone can join thousands of fans who elect to walk across the former Sixth Street Bridge (now named the "Roberto Clemente Bridge") that has been

BY THE NUMBERS

8—The number of losses with which the Pirates began the 1955 season—the worst-ever start in Bucs history.

closed off to vehicular traffic, amid shouting souvenir vendors, an occasional street musician, and skipping youngsters wearing Pirates shirts bearing the names and numbers of their favorite players.

Some seasoned fans pause out front and, with their eyes reflecting a legion of priceless memories, admire the statues of Clemente, Honus Wagner, and Willie Stargell. Once inside the gates, others stand next to the sculpture honoring Ralph Kiner; a few lean close to grasp the bronze copy of his giant hands holding a bat.

For those with a few extra bucks to spend, 69 luxury box suites with their own concourse level are available. For others on more restricted budgets, there are plenty of opportunities to visit one of the restaurants such as the "Outback in the Outfield" or former Pirate Manny Sanguillen's popular barbecue beyond the center-field stands.

PNC Park says to the good people of Pittsburgh that this franchise, a part of our community for more than a century, offers to the entire family a rich opportunity to watch a new history unfold before their eyes.

VOICES FROM ON HIGH

For many of us, our introductions to the Pittsburgh Pirates have come from listening to descriptions of games by Rosey Rowswell, Bob Prince, Lanny Frattare, and others who have sat behind microphones of WWSW, KDKA, and the Pirate Broadcast Network.

These people, for Pirates fans, are not merely announcers. They have become parts of our families. We've invited them into our homes and into our cars. We've celebrated with them during the terrific years; we hear the tears in their voices when the team comes so close but fails to win it all.

This chapter looks at the influence and personalities of these announcers. If you listen closely, perhaps you'll be able to hear once more the sound of their unforgettable voices.

PETUNIA PATCHES AND GREEN WEENIES

Modern-day baseball fans seldom are at a loss for information about their favorite teams or players. They're immersed in an avalanche of media coverage and instantaneous reports of happenings both on and off the field through reports on television, radio, and the Internet. The more sophisticated rooters can even download the latest scores on their cell phones. This generation, therefore, might have difficulty imagining what it was like to live at a time when sports news was available only through local newspapers. Depending on location of the game and circulation of the paper, it could take one or more days for game results to reach readers.

The Pittsburgh Pirates helped change all that. With the first airing of a Major League Baseball game on radio, the team opened the door to a new era of sports—live coverage—and the creation of a new celebrity known as the sportscaster.

Since then, the Pirates have been blessed with an array of colorful personalities behind the microphone.

Five memorable voices have graced Pittsburgh airways as lead announcers.

Harold Arlin—On August 5, 1921, a 25-year-old Westinghouse engineer-turned–radio announcer sat in a box seat along the first-base line at Pittsburgh's Forbes Field and made history. Arlin, in cooperation with radio station KDKA, described the play-by-play that afternoon, as the Pirates defeated the Philadelphia Phillies by a score of 8–5.

It was the first-ever broadcast of a Major League Baseball game.

Although it would be a quarter century before the Pirates hired a full-time broadcaster for all of its games, Harold Arlin was the Kit Carson of sportscasting. He paved the way for voices that would become icons of American culture: the rapid-fire delivery of Mel Allen, the southern drawl of Red Barber, the zany cheering of Harry Caray, the elegance and professionalism of Vin Scully, and, yes, the colorful yarns of Bob Prince. And who can forget the phrases "Holy Cow!"; "Going, Going, Gone!"; "How about that?"; "You can kiss it good-bye!"; or the cry of Russ Hodges in 1951 when Bobby Thomson smacked the Shot Heard 'Round the World: "The Giants win the pennant! The Giants win the pennant!"?

When Arlin carried a microphone and a converted telephone into Forbes Field in 1921, both the team and the radio station viewed the broadcast as an experiment. "I did this as a one-shot project," admitted Arlin years later. "Our broadcast, back then, at least, wasn't that big a deal. To tell the truth, our guys at KDKA didn't think that baseball would last on radio."

Radio, in fact, was in the kindergarten stage of development. KDKA's "studios" were housed under a portable canvas tent atop the downtown Westinghouse Building. Broadcasters had to cut away to silence when a train passed. KDKA, the first nonexperimental, licensed station, and the first to air programming on a regular basis, had been on the air for only nine months when Arlin attempted to make the game come alive in real time, painting pictures with words. Decades later, *Sports Illustrated* praised this groundbreaking event when it wrote, "Arlin's play-by-play demonstrated to the public that baseball could be brought into the American living room with immediacy and intimacy."

Before he died in 1986 at the age of 90, Arlin returned to the microphone for one last time on August 30, 1972. Arlin's grandson, Steve, had made it to the big leagues and was the starting pitcher that evening for the visiting San Diego Padres at Three Rivers Stadium. Pirates broadcaster Bob Prince invited the radio pioneer to sit next to him to watch the contest from the vantage point of the broadcast booth. Without any warning, when young

A rare glimpse of history came to those who witnessed 90-year-old Harold Arlin's return to the broadcast booth, at the invitation of Bob Prince, as he described young Steve Arlin's pitching performance when the Pirates hosted his grandson's San Diego Padres at Three Rivers Stadium on August 30, 1972.
(Photo courtesy of the National Baseball Hall of Fame)

Steve took the mound, Prince thrust the microphone in front of Arlin and asked: "Why not take over for a bit?"

For the next few innings, Arlin did just that. Those who were fortunate to see him that day claim they never saw a man look happier.

Aunt Minnie's Favorite Nephew might seem to be a strange label for anyone, let alone a broadcaster of baseball games. However, if you ask anyone who lived in Pittsburgh during the 1940s and '50s, he or she will quickly identify exactly to whom that title refers. It was none other than Albert Kennedy "Rosey" Rowswell.

Rowswell, a diminutive 5'6", 120 pounds, was the first full-time lead announcer for Pirates games. Beginning with Opening Day in 1936, Rowswell used a simple, homespun approach to describing games on stations WWSW and KDKA.

To the delight of the Forbes Field crowd, Rosey Rowswell escorts his mythical Aunt Minnie in a classic 1939 American Bantam convertible.

Rowswell was an unashamed hometown rooter for his Buccos. If a Pirates player made a poor play, or when the team was blown away by the opposition (something that often happened during his 19 years in the broadcast booth), he would moan, "Oh, my achin' back."

He coined some unique expressions that became familiar to regular listeners and completely baffled out-of-towners who might be listening to him for the first time. He described the strikeout of an opposing batter, for example, as "the old dipsey doodle." If a Pirate hit a ball for extra bases, it was a "doozey marooney."

He exclaimed his trademark call when a Pirate slugged a home run. In lieu of a simple "It's outta here" or some other trite statement, Rowswell summoned a mythical relative and shouted, "Raise the window, Aunt Minnie. Here she comes, right into your petunia patch!"

Rowswell did not enjoy traveling away from home for days at a time. Instead of joining the team on road trips, he re-created the games while sitting in front of a Teletype machine at the local radio station. From the Western Union relay setup, he read a cryptic note that would say, for example, "Westlake singles to center." Rosey would then place his imagination into overdrive as he created a picture of something he could not see. He described, for instance, how the ball was lined over second base, just out of the reach of the diving second baseman, who then lay on the ground pounding the dirt with his fist in frustration at missing the ball.

When a Pirate hit a home run, the theatrics increased. When Rowswell would alert them that he was about to give his "Raise the window, Aunt Minnie" call, his sidekick, Jack Craddock (until he resigned in 1947), and afterward, the flashy Bob Prince, would hold a tray heaped with glass, bolts, nuts, and anything else that simulated the sound of a breaking window pane, and let it all drop on a table in front of the microphone. Rosey then sighed, "She never made it."

Rosey Rowswell was a popular after-dinner speaker who endeared audiences with his down-home humor and original poetry.

When he died on February 6, 1955, at age 71, Pittsburghers responded en masse. Columnist Edwin Beacher wrote, "Crowds lined both sides of Neville Street for a block, outside the Samson Funeral Home, where eight rooms had been filled to overflowing for the services. Outside, old women wearing babushkas mourned side by side with bobby soxers, bewhiskered old timers and school children toting book bags and lunch boxes. Hundreds of others gathered at Allegheny Cemetery as the late afternoon sun faded into the hillside; there to see him laid to rest on this hillside facing west, which Rosey had selected."

The Gunner is a handle that applies to only one man—Bob Prince. Following the death of Rosey Rowswell, Prince assumed his rightful place as the Pirates' number one announcer.

Perhaps the best way to describe this man, whose trademarks were his horn-rimmed eyeglasses and flashy sport coats, is to say that he was a boy in a man's body. Always looking for opportunities to push the envelope, Prince was never afraid to see just how far he could go to make a point, or to add another level of entertainment to his broadcasts.

When he first ventured into the world of broadcasting, a few of his colleagues considered him opinionated and a bit of a loudmouth. Prince, a dropout of Harvard Law School, actually agreed with his critics but said he did whatever it took to get himself recognized around the Pittsburgh area. With the resignation of Jack Craddock following the '47 season, Prince applied for, and won, the slot as the sidekick to Rowswell.

Initially, the combination of these two contrasting personalities resembled water and oil. Rowswell never touched alcohol and was a quiet, devout Methodist who, following a broadcast, drove straight home. Prince, on the other hand, knew every bar in downtown Pittsburgh and was a flirt (although a devoted family man who raised two children with his wife of 44 years, Betty). Gradually, the two broadcasters complemented each other and became close friends.

Like his predecessor, Prince honed an atypical way of describing plays. A ball driven by a Pirate between the outfielders was a "tweener." When a baseball bounced high off the artificial turf of

Three Rivers Stadium, it was a "bug on the rug." For a home run, Prince exclaimed, "You can kiss it good-bye!" If the Pirates eked out a win in the last inning, he sighed with an aura of satirical confidence, "We had 'em all the way."

His most outlandish gimmick was a hand-held prop. During the 1966 campaign, if a visiting team started a rally, Prince devised a unique way to place a "curse" on the opponents by sticking a hunk of plastic shaped like a hot dog out of the broadcast booth. He painted it a bright kelly green. Fans and media referred to this unusual object as the "Green Weenie."

Logic said something like this would never work. However, if the opposition started to collect a few hits in one inning, fans would holler from the stands, "Hey, Bob, get your Green Weenie!" Prince responded by pointing the plastic artifact at the batter wearing the gray uniform. The crowd cheered. Suddenly, the visiting players (perhaps because they were "psyched out") stopped hitting.

Prince grew extremely close to the ballplayers. He became especially fond of Roberto Clemente, a talented native of Puerto Rico, who was shy and unable to communicate in English as well as some people thought he should. Many in the local media were often unkind in their remarks about the young right fielder. Prince adopted a more positive approach and became one of Clemente's most enthusiastic fans. If Clemente made a spectacular catch in the outfield or got a timely hit, Prince urged his listeners to shout, "*Arriba! Arriba!*" which, in Spanish, is an interjection used to express pleasure, approval, or elation.

As if Prince's life were scripted as a Greek tragedy, the Gunner's strength became his greatest weakness. His flamboyant disregard for the established norm eventually wore thin with Westinghouse Broadcasting, which had recently purchased the rights to the Pirates broadcast. His bosses grew increasingly irritated at his habit of drifting away from the action on the field and spinning yarns about Pirates of bygone eras. Their pleas to alter his style fell on deaf ears.

Following the 1975 season, Westinghouse Broadcasting and Pirates general manager Joe L. Brown announced that Prince would not return for a 29th year as a Bucs broadcaster.

Pirates fans rebelled. Their outcries inspired more than 10,000 loyal fans to line the streets on November 5 of that year to watch a downtown parade honoring Prince. Pirates management, however, remained unmoved.

Prince tried other ventures, including a one-season stint as a broadcaster with the Houston Astros, but he was unable to regain his former status.

Ten years later, Prince, a pack-a-day smoker, was diagnosed with mouth cancer. Shortly following a stay in the hospital, he was invited back as a Pirates broadcaster. The illness, unfortunately, had already taken its toll. On May 3, 1985, he resumed his place behind the microphone but was able to broadcast only two innings. He had strength enough for two more games before returning to the hospital and succumbing to the cancer on June 10.

The next year, Prince was honored posthumously with the Ford C. Frick Award, which enshrined him in the writers and broadcasters wing of the Baseball Hall of Fame in Cooperstown.

Milo Hamilton was another Pirates broadcaster who would receive the Ford C. Frick Award, in 1992. He was a veteran announcer who had the distinction of calling Hank Aaron's 715th home-run shot in '74. Well respected in the industry, he described the action of a game in a cool, relaxed, and dispassionate style.

Regrettably for him, while in Pittsburgh from 1976 to 1979, he was a man who was in the wrong place at the wrong time.

Brought in to replace the legendary Bob Prince, Hamilton had an uphill fight beginning with the first words he uttered from the booth. Unlike the flamboyant style of arm-waving enthusiasm employed by Prince, Hamilton was a reserved reporter who used proper English at all times. He refused to lose himself in hyperbole and could never be accused of "cheerleading" from his seat in the second deck behind home plate at Three Rivers Stadium. In short, he was exactly the kind of announcer the new broadcast-rights owners sought to replace Prince.

Pittsburgh fans, however, didn't buy it, or him. Most of their negative feelings were by-products of the backlash resulting from

WHY "THE GUNNER"?

Not long ago, nicknames were common among baseball personalities. Veteran fans know exactly about whom you were speaking if you mentioned the names of "Babe," "Duke," "Pee Wee," "Dizzy," "Rocket," and "The Man."

The Pirates, too, have had their share of nicknames: "Rabbit," "Kiki," "Pie," "Pops," "Arky," "Rip," "Cobra," and "Deacon."

Rarely, however, have we heard of a broadcaster who is so identified with a nickname that even the modern fan recognizes the man.

Bob Prince was one of those exceptions. And the name with which he will always be identified is "Gunner."

Why was he branded with this name? Two reasons are given, both of which are logical.

The first is an apt description of his rapid-fire delivery. It seems that Prince squeezed more words into a minute's commentary than most people could produce in two or three times that amount of time.

The second involved the following report told by Prince himself: Following a spring-training game in Florida on an Easter Sunday, Prince, as was his custom, visited a local watering hole with his on-the-air partner Jim Woods. Prince, a gregarious personality, struck up a conversation with a woman seated on the stool next to him. It was an innocent dialogue; nothing that was said was out of line, according to Woods.

After a while, the woman departed the scene. Prince and Woods were just about ready to call it a night when, suddenly, the woman's husband stormed into the bar while grasping a shotgun. He approached Prince and pointed the weapon at his nose. In a voice loud enough to be heard by everyone in the establishment, the irate husband accused Prince of flirting with his wife.

Prince reached into his grab bag of clever remarks and quickly convinced the steaming mate that there must have been a huge mistake. Prince pointed out that obviously the man's wife left in a hurry just to be home with the man she loved. The husband accepted Prince's explanation and quietly retreated out the door.

The next day, while on the air, Woods casually referred to Prince as "Gunner." The listening audience didn't know the full implication of the label. Nonetheless, it stuck.

the firing of Prince—an announcer they had grown to love over the past 28 years.

To Hamilton's credit, he didn't strike back in anger. Instead, whenever possible, he remained eager to share his experience in broadcasting with others. He took under his wing a young sportscaster from Rochester, New York, Lanny Frattare, and groomed him on many of the technical aspects of describing play-by-play.

"I put up with all the negativity for two years," said Hamilton, who didn't intend to wait it out. Before his fourth season, he had enough. "I told my wife in spring training that this would be my last year. The fans were great, but the Pittsburgh media just couldn't understand how anybody could replace Bob Prince. And probably they were right."

After Hamilton left the Pirates, he moved to Chicago to broadcast the Cubs games, then to Houston as the lead announcer for the Astros.

Lanny Frattare has been the lead play-by-play man for the Bucs since 1980 and a member of the broadcast team since 1976, giving him the record for broadcasting the most games in Pirates history.

Frattare shuns the designation "Voice of the Pirates" in deference to his longtime friend and mentor, Bob Prince, who gave him his first exposure behind a Pirates microphone back in '75, when Frattare called games for the Pirates' Triple-A affiliate in Charleston, West Virginia.

A 1970 graduate of Ithaca (NY) College, Frattare still shakes his head in amazement at how quickly he was thrust onto the big-league scene. Little did he know that Prince would be fired less than a year following Frattare's debut in the Pirates booth. Apparently, he left enough of a positive impression, and the Pittsburgh club invited him back to team with Milo Hamilton in 1976.

"Milo shielded me from much of the criticism he received," Frattare remembered. As a result, Frattare was never linked with Hamilton when Pirates fans rebelled against the man who replaced Bob Prince.

He describes accurately the action of the ballgame, yet there's no mistake that, with each inning, he is cheering for a Pirates victory. His passion is transparent, although he never allows himself to opine about in-house controversies, especially when they involved some of his close friends—managers Jim Leyland and Gene Lamont, for example.

Frattare, as did some of those who preceded him, developed his own phrases while describing a game. One of his best-known phrases echoes one coined by Bob Prince following every Pirates victory. Frattare's version is: "There was noooooooooooo doubt about it!"

Another unique call for Frattare is when a Pirate slams a home run. As the ball heads toward the outfield wall, Frattare shouts as words of encouragement, "Go, ball! Get outta here!"

One of the secrets to Frattare's longevity with the team is his closeness with ballplayers. He is never afraid to mingle with them and get to know them personally. While on the air, Frattare has never been critical of a player or manager who made a mental or physical error on the field. He might point out the mistake but will never pass judgment.

Another "plus" on the Frattare résumé is that he constantly speaks highly of his broadcast partners in the booth—Steve Blass, Greg Brown, Bob Walk, and John Wehner. "I believe the strength of our broadcast team is rooted in the fact that we help each other play to our strengths," he said.

Frattare's outstanding work in the community includes hosting the annual Family Links Golf Classic, which has raised nearly $2 million over the past 20-plus years in support of more than 32,000 children, families, and mentally challenged individuals who are served each year by the event.

BY THE NUMBERS

10—Number of times Max Carey led the league in stolen bases (1913, 1915, 1916, 1917, 1918, 1920, 1922, 1923, 1924, 1925).

One might conclude that Frattare ranks among the most highly regarded professionals in his field. As a result, he's expected to remain as the Pirates lead announcer for as long as he wants the job.

SIDEKICKS AND COLOR GUYS

There are two kinds of baseball announcers—radio broadcasters and television commentators. With each comes a profound difference in his or her objective.

For the listeners who have their car radios tuned to a Pirates broadcast as they fight the traffic along Route 19, the radio broadcaster paints a picture with words of what is happening on the field. The radio broadcaster describes the intimidating glare in the eyes of a pitcher, as he seems to dare a batter to get a piece of his fastball. The radio broadcaster attempts to allow the listener to see the potential base-stealer get a late start off first, only to get thrown out on a "bang-bang" play at second.

The television commentator is someone who attempts to add to what the viewer sees on a 21-inch screen in the family den or on monstrous HD models at a local watering hole. While the radio broadcaster paints the picture with words, the television commentator provides an appropriate frame around the picture that's before the viewer.

We Pittsburghers have been blessed with announcers who have become a part of our lives in a positive way. When the team struggles, with a word of comfort or a touch of humor, they remind us that we're all in this together. When the Pirates emerge victorious, the announcers let us know that it is permissible to let our emotions overflow through hand-clapping, cork-popping, and singing of silly songs.

The Bucs' lead announcers have received the majority of accolades. However, as all of them would admit, they owe their successes, to a large part, to the sidekicks who provide balance to their commentaries and additional color to descriptions of the action on the diamond.

Here's a salute to some of the Pirates fans' favorites.

Jim "Possum" Woods (1958–1969)

Yankees great Whitey Ford jokingly nicknamed Jim Woods "Possum" because, he said, the announcer, with his short-cut white hair, reminded him of the rodent. Woods was a superb broadcaster whose smooth, gravel-voiced delivery gave a harmonious contrast to the rapid-fire delivery of Bob Prince.

On the air, neither Prince nor Woods attempted to "one-up" the other with caustic remarks. They acted as two good friends would. And this was no act. They truly enjoyed each other's company in the broadcast booth and at an occasional after-game rendezvous at a nearby club.

Following 12 years behind the microphone on the Pirate Broadcast Network, Woods took positions as a color commentator with St. Louis, Oakland, and the Boston Red Sox. His days in Pittsburgh, he said to his dying day, were the most cherished.

Nellie King (1967–1975)

When he was a relief pitcher for the Pirates (1954–1957), Nelson King won a total of seven games. During that time, he was able to gain many more laughs from his teammates.

Known as the team prankster, King was willing to do things that others may have only considered. One was the time in 1956 when, on a road trip, slugger Dale Long had not appeared by the time the bus was ready to leave for the stadium. Long was in the midst of his record-breaking eight-game home-run streak and the only Pirate providing any punch in the lineup that year. Instead of allowing the bus to leave without their most valuable teammate, King lay his 6'6" frame in front of the wheels of the vehicle.

A sore arm caused King to retire from the game prematurely. He elected, then, to enter the field of broadcasting, first in some of the smaller communities surrounding the 'Burgh. Then in 1967 he was invited to join Bob Prince and Jim Woods as the third man in the booth. When Woods chose to go his separate way, and Gene Osborn—who lasted only one year—left the Pittsburgh booth, King was paired with Prince beginning in 1971.

The smooth-talking King was a pleasant complement to the gregarious Prince, and the two became close friends.

King unfortunately became the wrong man in the wrong place at the wrong time, and he was a casualty with the firing of Prince in 1975.

Following his tenure with the Pirates, King became affiliated with Duquesne University and an active member of the Pirates' Alumni Association. Today, he's a popular speaker at banquets and other baseball gatherings.

Nellie Briles (1979–1980)

Had it not been for his sharp-breaking curveball and pinpoint control, Nelson Briles may have become a success in show business. He had matinee-idol looks, a remarkable stage appearance, and a singing voice that would be the envy of most opera producers.

Following his 14 years in the big leagues, three of which were with the Pirates (1971–1973, including a brilliant two-hit shutout of Baltimore in Game 5 of the 1971 World Series), Briles entered

Two of the Pirates all-time favorite announcers, Nellie Briles (left) and Steve Blass (right), appear to be competing in an ugly-shirt contest as they confer with former Pirates manager Jim Leyland.

the arena of broadcasting. He didn't just walk into a position; he had to "sell" himself.

Briles noticed while watching Pirates games on KDKA-TV that the broadcast might be improved were someone in the booth who had "been there." So, Briles called the producer and sought to join the team as a color analyst.

"We don't have color analysts," came the rather terse reply.

"Well, I'd make a good one," said Briles.

"The bottom line is that we can't afford one," admitted the producer.

"I'll work for free," said Briles.

That was an offer that jived with the program's budget, so the producer offered to bring Briles aboard for a few broadcasts just to see how it would work out.

It worked great. For two seasons, he entertained Pirates audiences with his quips and anecdotes. Afterward, he became a vice president with the club for corporate projects and president of the Alumni Association.

Like the hero in one of his favorite operas, Briles died of an unexpected heart attack while golfing at an Alumni Association gathering in Orlando. He was only 61 years old.

Jim Rooker (1981–1993)

Another former pitcher, Jim Rooker, spent eight years with the Pirates from 1973 to 1980. He became best known not for his 103–109 record during his 13-year big-league career, but for his rather pointed, outspoken comments while an announcer with the Pirates.

The one comment for which he will be remembered by everyone who had heard it, came during a broadcast in Philadelphia on June 8, 1989, when, behind the pitching of the steady Bob Walk, the Bucs jumped to a 10–0 lead in the first inning. "If we lose this one," said a confident Rooker, "I'll *walk* back to Pittsburgh."

As if scripted by a "B" movie producer, the Phillies chipped away. With the game tied 11–11 in the eighth, Philadelphia's Darren Daulton smacked a two-run single to put the opposition ahead to stay.

Rooker had to live up to his promise. During the off-season, the humbled announcer took a 13-day, 305-mile walk for charity from the City of Brotherly Love to Pittsburgh. As he soaked his blistering feet at the end of his journey, he was delighted to learn that he had gathered more than $81,000 in donations for his effort.

Steve Blass (1983–Present)

Question: Could anything endear someone more to a Pittsburgh Pirates fan than spending 10 years with the club, compiling an impressive 103–76 record with a 3.63 ERA, and being a hero who pitched a four-hit, 2–1 victory over Baltimore in Game 7 of the 1971 World Series?

Strangely enough, the answer is yes—when it applies to broadcaster Steve Blass.

Since 1983, this jovial Connecticut Yankee has won the hearts of Pittsburghers with his delicious sense of humor. One of his colleagues, Greg Brown, says, "Steve Blass has an incredibly quick wit. His storytelling ability is unmatched. He is one of the funniest people I've ever met."

In 2005, Blass elected to eschew traveling with the team and remain at home during the season to spend more time with his family. He also became more focused on his role as a spokesman for the Pirates Alumni Association.

Bob Walk (1994–Present)

Following a 14-year career as a major league pitcher, 10 of them (1984–1993) with the Pirates, Robert Vernon Walk decided it wasn't his native Van Nuys, California, that was his real home; it was Pittsburgh.

Joining the team of Lanny Frattare, Steve Blass, and fellow newcomer Greg Brown, Walk replaced Jim Rooker—the man who, ironically, promised to walk Route 30 between Philadelphia and Pittsburgh, while Walk was staked to a 10–0 lead in the opening frame of a contest at Veterans Stadium.

Walk learned the power of the media one evening when he complained, on the air, that there was no coffee available in the broadcast booth. The next day, he and his team were deluged with gifts of ground coffee—enough to last for the remainder of the season.

Over the years, Walk has graduated from a color man who adds an occasional remark to a full-blown announcer who could, if necessary, handle with ease an entire game solo.

Today, his colleagues and a new generation of fans appreciate the kind of insights that can be given only by a former player.

Greg Brown (1994–Present)

Greg Brown, a native of Mechanicsburg, Pennsylvania, has been called by many fans in the Pittsburgh area "the best number two man in the history of the franchise."

This praise is not mere hyperbole. Playing second banana to the articulate Lanny Frattare seems to be natural to Brown. The young man, who wore a lot of hats with the Pirates organization (from assistant clubhouse manager to donning the costume of the Pirate mascot), lays back and allows the lead announcer to deliver most of the comments about the action on the field. When appropriate, he'll add a phrase or comment that's genuinely compelling.

Perhaps the most pointed lines he ever delivered were those that could never have been scripted. One instance happened on May 28, 2004, during the second game of a doubleheader at PNC Park against Chicago. Pirates third baseman Rob Mackowiak had not slept all the night before, as his wife had given birth to their first child—a son they named Garrett. With the Bucs behind by two runs in the ninth inning and with a man on, a sleepy Mackowiak stepped to the plate and promptly drilled a long drive deep into the right-field stands. As the ball headed over the 21-foot wall in right field, Brown yelled, "Garrett, your father has just tied this game."

Could anyone have said it better?

John Wehner (2005–Present)

With apologies to the popular television program *Jeopardy!*, the answer is: "Who is John Wehner?"

The question is: "He was the last person ever to hit a home run at Three Rivers Stadium."

BY THE NUMBERS

16—Number of consecutive games the eventual World Series champion Pirates won in 1909, a record for the club.

An alternative question could be: "He made the last out as a batter at Three Rivers Stadium."

Wehner did both during the last game at the Pirates' former home turf on the evening of October 1, 2000, during a disappointing 10–9 loss to the Cubs.

A graduate of Carrick High School in his native Pittsburgh, Wehner was signed by the Pirates on five separate occasions (1988, 1999, 2000, January 2001, and August 2001). In 11 major league seasons, he played for two teams (Pirates and Marlins) and won a World Series ring because he was brought into one game as a defensive replacement during the 1997 National League Division Series when he was with Florida.

When Steve Blass asked to be excused from broadcasting road games for the Bucs, Wehner was brought on board as a color analyst for the Fox Sports Network in 2005.

Wehner brings with him a folksy, yet authoritative approach to the game—two things Pirates fans and management appreciate.

MEMORABLE LINES BY PIRATES BROADCASTERS

Throughout history, certain people are associated with specific expressions. In fact, when you hear particular sayings, you automatically get a mental image of the person who delivered those lines.

The rallying cry "I have a dream" will always be associated with Dr. Martin Luther King Jr. Who can ever forget President John F. Kennedy's plea, "Ask not what your country can do for you; ask what you can do for your country"?

Baseball's on-air commentators also have discovered clever ways of expressing routine happenings on a ball field, giving us a different look at some things we've seen all of our lives.

Here is a sample of memorable comments by Pittsburgh Pirates broadcasters that have captured our fancy:

"When he pitches, it's like a barnful of owls coming at you."
—Steve Blass, describing a pitcher's unorthodox delivery

"He should have been better, pitching on 3,195 days rest."
—Steve Blass in 1995, on Pittsburgh replacement pitcher Jimmy Boudreau, who last played professionally in 1986

"He's pitching as if he was double-parked."
—Bob Walk, describing a visiting pitcher's quickness in delivering pitches

"Garrett, your father has just tied this game."
—Greg Brown, when calling a home-run shot by Rob Mackowiak on the afternoon of May 28, 2004, after the young Pirates third baseman had spent a sleepless night at the hospital when his first child—Garrett—was born

"We'll be back in a moment with the wrap-up of the game."
—The only comment by Bob Prince after a game-winning home run by the Cardinals' Stan Musial in St. Louis

"There are a reported 15,000 people at the game this afternoon. If that's true, then at least 12,000 of them are disguised as empty seats."
—Jim Woods, commenting on a small crowd at Forbes Field

"He was out by a gnat's eyelash."
—Bob Prince, describing a close play at first

"Raise the window, Aunt Minnie. Here she comes, right in your petunia patch."
—Rosey Rowswell's description of a Pirates home run

"Oh, my achin' back."
—Rosey Rowswell, whenever the Pirates were losing (which was quite often during his tenure)

"There was noooooooooooo doubt about it."
—Lanny Frattare, immediately after the final out of a Pirates victory

15 MINUTES OF FAME

Pittsburgh's own Andy Warhol once proclaimed, "In the future, everybody will be famous for 15 minutes." The famed pop artist referred to the fleeting condition known as "celebrity" that attaches to a person who's thrust instantly into the limelight, then, just as quickly, passes from view once the public's attention span has been exhausted. Warhol's pronouncement is often used in reference to figures in the entertainment industry, as well as in other areas of popular culture, including Major League Baseball.

Joining the cast of characters in the latter group are four Pirates who personify Warhol's familiar pronouncement.

Paul Pettit had shown remarkable talent as a pitcher. His experience, however, was limited to his appearances for Narbonne High School in Lomita, California.

For some reason known only to the team's front office, Pirates scouts in 1950 signed the 18-year-old Pettit to a big-league contract that came with a bonus check for $100,000 attached. It was the most money ever paid to a rookie in the history of the game.

Granted, a bonus that size might never create headlines in today's economy. In 1950, however, $100,000 was more than 20 times the average yearly salary paid to a schoolteacher. This first player ever to be called a "bonus baby" was the talk of Pittsburgh.

The local media were excited about the prospect, who, some claimed, would make the Pirates genuine contenders. Sportswriters for Pittsburgh's three newspapers—the *Pittsburgh Post-Gazette,* the *Pittsburgh Sun-Telegraph,* and *The Pittsburgh Press*—set aside their anointing oil long enough to compete for fresh angles about the young phenom. Bucs broadcaster Rosey Rowswell, who refused to travel with the team, drove to Florida to air a special program direct from spring training in February 1951, during which he described the pitches tossed by the youngster in batting practice.

Pettit had the stuff required of a major league pitcher: a fastball that was in the mid-90s and a pretty good curve. He certainly looked great on paper. Unfortunately, once an experienced hitter stepped to the plate, the 6'2" southpaw became reduced to less than average. Not only was he unable to overpower hitters, but he also lacked control.

He pitched just 2⅔ innings in 1951, with no decisions. After a year of seasoning in the minors, he appeared in 10 games during the 1953 season with the Pirates, going 1–2.

Pettit, however, loved baseball and caught the attention of several other scouts while in the minors. He hit .320 for the Hollywood Stars in 1952 and compiled a 15–8 record on the mound. He showed home-run power in both the California League and the Mexican League.

While in the Pacific Coast League, in 1958 Pettit replaced Dick Stuart in right field after the slugger was brought up to the parent club in Pittsburgh.

Pettit played a few more years in organized baseball, although never in the big leagues, before he went back to school, earned a master's degree, and returned to his roots as a teacher and coach in Lomita, California.

Ted Beard was a sure-handed outfielder with the Indianapolis Indians—the Pirates' Triple-A farm team. One month before the close of the 1948 regular season, Pirates owner Frank McKinney announced that he was calling up the star right fielder, who hit .301 with 85 RBIs and led the league in triples (17), runs (131), and walks (128).

During his seven seasons in the majors, five of which were with the Pirates, Beard compiled a rather minuscule average of

.198, not exactly a spectacular legacy for an outfielder. But, on July 16, 1950, during the nightcap of a Sunday doubleheader in Forbes Field, Beard had his one glorious moment of fame. While never known as a consistent home-run hitter (he hit a grand total of six his entire career), the 5'8", 165-pounder got hold of an inside pitch from Boston Braves pitcher Bob Hall and sent the ball high and deep to right field. Right fielder Tommy Holmes took one step back toward the screen and stopped to watch in amazement as the ball cleared not only the screen, but also the 86-foot roof of the right-field stands.

For a brief moment, the fans seated in the stands sat in shocked silence. Then they rose to their feet and erupted with applause. As Beard circled the bases, many onlookers shook their heads in disbelief. Who would have believed that Beard could have hit a ball over the roof? The last person, and only person, to do that before Beard was the legendary Babe Ruth who, on May 25, 1935, hit three homers while a player for the Braves. The blast over the roof was the last of his career—number 714.

For the record, eight others have hit hit four-baggers over the roof. They were Mickey Mantle, Wally Moon, Bob Skinner (2), Eddie Mathews (2), Jerry Lynch, Rusty Staub, Willie McCovey, and Willie Stargell (7).

Dino Restelli was 24 years old when he broke into the big leagues on June 14, 1949, with the Pittsburgh Pirates. Seldom in the history of Major League Baseball have we seen someone who made such an immediate impact on the sport.

In his first 12 games with the Bucs, the muscular Italian American slammed seven home runs. Furthermore, Restelli endeared himself to fans when he would pull out a large, red, polka-dot handkerchief from his hip pocket and use it to clean the thick eyeglasses he wore each game

In less than two weeks, Restelli, it appeared, had replaced Ralph Kiner as the idol of Pirates fans. Even the national media became caught up in the hype. The July 4, 1949, edition of *Time* magazine carried this description of Restelli: "a rawboned young man with powerful arms, bushy eyebrows and a sunny disposition. Like baseball's famed DiMaggio brothers, he comes from San

BY THE NUMBERS

23—The number of games the Pittsburgh squad (then called the Alleghenies) lost in 1890—a team record.

Francisco's sandlots. A fortnight ago he got into the lineup as an outfielder and began cannonading the fences as few pea-green rookies ever had before."

Almost overnight, things turned sour. Opposing pitchers discovered a fatal flaw in Restelli's hitting attack. He could not hit a major league curveball. Before the ink had dried on the newspaper editorials nominating him as a surefire candidate for the Hall of Fame, Restelli slumped miserably, ending the season with 12 home runs and a .250 average. Kiner quietly moved back onto his throne as Pittsburgh's king of swat.

After his splash in '49, Restelli did not even make the team in spring training the next year. Pittsburgh called him back in 1951 for 21 games before selling him to the Washington Senators.

Restelli played in only 93 big-league games and never appeared again at the major league level. After serving as a police officer in California, he died on August 8, 2006.

Hal Smith is perhaps the best example of Andy Warhol's concept of fleeting fame. Smith came to the Pirates from Kansas City prior to the 1960 campaign. His primary role was to serve as a backup for catcher Smoky Burgess.

He served his team well in that capacity. A superb defensive catcher, he could be called on in late innings to help preserve leads or to work behind the plate during one game of a doubleheader. As a pinch-hitter, he came through with timely hits that enabled the Bucs to win the league championship.

Smith's brush with genuine fame came in that year's World Series, and it lasted exactly one inning. It was Hal Smith's three-run line drive over the wall in the eighth inning of Game 7 in the 1960 World Series, off pitcher Jim Coates, that gave the Bucs a temporary 9–7 lead over the highly favored New York Yankees.

Broadcaster Chuck Thompson, caught up in the frenzy of the screaming fans, shouted to the nation, "Forbes Field has just become an outdoor insane asylum." Pirates general manager Joe L. Brown said that of all his experiences in baseball, this was his most exciting moment.

The backup catcher's blast seemingly nailed the Series for Pittsburgh.

Alas, fate would not be kind to Smith. Timely hitting and heads-up base running by Mickey Mantle and company tied the score in the top of the ninth. Taking Smith's place as the hero on October 13, 1960, was Bill Mazeroski who, in the next inning, hit the home run that we've all seen replayed hundreds of times.

What about Smith's dramatic clout? It became the "forgotten home run," and the backup catcher was reduced to a World Series footnote.

Smith had an off-season in 1961. He was left unprotected for the expansion draft the next winter and was claimed by the newly formed Houston Colt 45's; he retired from baseball in 1964 after a 10-year career.

Most fans might not consider Smith as one of the all-time greats. But for those Pirates fans who were around during the 1960 World Series and remember that majestic Game 7, they'll never forget the backup catcher who, with one swing of a bat, made the most of Andy Warhol's predicted 15 minutes of fame.

BY THE NUMBERS

44—Babe Adam's age in 1926. Not yet ready to book a room in a retirement home, he became the oldest player to play for the team. Adams ended the season with a 2–3 record and a 6.14 ERA.

ALL-TIME PIRATES GREATS

Getting to the major leagues is a dream come true for every ballplayer who signs a professional contract. For a select few, however, there's another level of success—to be among the best who ever played the game.

Of the Pittsburgh Pirates players who have donned the black and gold, several have been elected into the Hall of Fame, nine have had their numbers retired, and four—Honus Wagner, Roberto Clemente, Willie Stargell, and Ralph Kiner—have sculptures in their honor at PNC Park.

The following pages constitute a tribute to the "best of the best" for the Pittsburgh Pirates.

PIRATES HALL OF FAMERS

In their long and glorious history, the Pittsburgh Pirates have had their fair share of players who were inducted into the Baseball Hall of Fame in Cooperstown, New York. The 11 Buccos who spent most or all of their careers in Pirates uniforms and have a plaque dedicated to their excellence are:

Johannes P. "Honus" Wagner (1936)

If Honus Wagner were a painting, he would be hanging in the Louvre. This hometown product from nearby Carnegie,

Pennsylvania, racked up a pile of incredible statistics over a career that spanned 21 seasons (1897–1917).

The barrel-chested, bowlegged shortstop hit better than .300 in 15 consecutive campaigns and led the National League in batting eight times, slugging six times, RBIs five times, doubles seven times, and runs scored twice. He stole 722 bases and compiled a .327 average—better than any shortstop in the history of Major League Baseball.

The Flying Dutchman played in nearly 2,800 big-league games with the Louisville Colonels and Pittsburgh Pirates. He amassed 3,415 hits, 640 doubles, 252 triples, 101 home runs, 1,732 RBIs, and 1,736 runs scored.

A little-known fact is that Wagner even pitched in two games—a total of eight innings—with a 0.00 ERA.

To say that Wagner was the greatest shortstop of all time may, in itself, be an understatement. Some renowned baseball experts, including John McGraw, Branch Rickey, and Ed Barrow—all of whom saw both Wagner and Babe Ruth during their heydays—cited Wagner as the greatest ever. Period.

Following his retirement from baseball, Wagner remained in the Pittsburgh area lending his name to a downtown sporting goods store and serving as a Pirates coach (1933–1952). Less than eight months prior to his death in 1955, Wagner got to attend the dedication of his statue that was placed outside Forbes Field and was since moved to Three Rivers Stadium, then to PNC Park.

It should come as no surprise that Wagner was one of the five original inductees into the Hall of Fame, along with Babe Ruth, Ty Cobb, Walter Johnson, and Christy Mathewson.

Fred Clarke (1945)

Fred Clarke joins this list of Pirates in the Hall of Fame by acclimation. Although his plaque in Cooperstown does not sport the famous Pirates *P*, there is no persuasive argument to convince baseball historians that this native of Winterset, Iowa, was not first and foremost a Pittsburgh Pirate.

Clarke, in fact, could arguably be chosen for the Hall as either a player or a manager.

He was a player/manager when he was part of the Louisville Colonels and joined the Pirates when the two teams merged after the National League cut back from 12 teams to eight following the 1899 season.

Through 21 years as an outfielder, Clarke registered 2,672 hits, batted a career .312, and played in two World Series (1903 and 1909).

His managerial accomplishments are covered in the appropriate section of this book, but it's fair to conclude that he was one of the most innovative people ever to guide a team. He was responsible for creating a tarpaulin that, with the help of his patented pulley system, could be rolled onto an infield during a storm, thus saving the surface for play once the rains ceased. Also, he devised "flipable" smoked glasses that a player could clip onto the bill of his cap and, in the event of a glaring sun, with one flick of the finger, let the shades fall over his eyes, resulting in better vision.

Clarke died in 1960 at age 87.

Harold J. "Pie" Traynor (1948)

When he was just five years old growing up in Framingham, Massachusetts, little Harold Traynor already knew what he wanted to do in life. When anyone asked, "What do you want to be when you grow up?" the youngster, who had a passion for pie (hence, his nickname), quickly responded, "A baseball player."

That vision stuck with him as he played ball in the minor leagues in New England and impressed the Pirates scouts who signed him to a contract. It was the start of a 17-year career with the Bucs that began in 1920.

In his first two years with the club, Traynor was tagged as a shortstop. However, he failed to show Hall of Fame credentials when he committed one error after another. Following more seasoning in the minors and solid coaching, the muscular infielder was moved to his rightful position at third base. It was there he developed into the prototypical player at the hot corner. As he matured at that position, he turned in some spectacular plays that led one reporter to write, "Yesterday, an opposing batter hit a double down the left-field line, and Pie Traynor threw him out at first."

Although not a power hitter (he hit 58 homers his entire career), he nevertheless hit plenty of double and triples, driving in 100 or more runs during seven seasons.

A lifetime .320 hitter, Traynor became a player/manager toward the end of the 1934 campaign, but he saw limited duty as a player due to injuries.

After compiling a 457–406 record at the helm, Traynor turned to broadcasting as the host of a local sports show and a goodwill ambassador for the Pirates. He also served as a scout and as an instructor at Bucs tryout camps.

Few people were as beloved in Pittsburgh as was Traynor when he died in 1972 at 73 years of age.

Paul "Big Poison" Waner (1952)

A man standing at 5'8" and weighing 153 pounds would hardly seem to be a candidate for the nickname Big Poison, but Paul Waner was an athlete who compressed a lot of raw talent inside his body and possessed a drive that turned logic inside out. He was a baseball player who won three batting titles and collected 200 or more hits in eight seasons. In addition, he led the National League twice in hits, three times in batting average, twice in doubles, and twice in triples. During his 15 years with the Pirates (1926–1940), he was selected an All-Star four times in the first five years of the midsummer classic's existence.

The left-hand-hitting native of Harrah, Oklahoma, was a master at controlling the bat. Seldom did he go down swinging; his career walks outnumbered his strikeouts, 1,091 to 376.

Like many of the rugged ballplayers of his era, Paul Waner was accustomed to drinking heavily, especially on the long train trips to away games. Rumors flourished during his playing days that Waner sometimes went onto the playing field while nearly intoxicated. If so, it never seemed to affect him. Even someone with the experience of Casey Stengel called Waner "the greatest right fielder I ever saw."

After leaving the Pirates, Waner played for the Brooklyn Dodgers and Boston Braves, then had a few at-bats with the New York Yankees.

Waner retired as a big-league player in 1945 after collecting 3,152 hits and compiling a career .333 batting average. He then coached for the Cardinals and the Phillies, and even played a few sandlot games for the local Dormont baseball team in suburban Pittsburgh.

Waner died in 1965 at age 62 in Sarasota, Florida.

In all of baseball, seldom has there been a combination of talent in two brothers as with the Pirates Paul Waner and Lloyd Waner—both of whom eventually were elected to the Hall of Fame.

Max Carey (1961)

He started out wanting to be a Lutheran pastor, and he made his mark in life as an evangelist for Major League Baseball. Maximilian Carey compiled a .285 average with 2,665 hits over a 20-year career, 17 of which (1910–1926) were with the Pirates.

A speedster, this outfielder led the National League in stolen bases 10 times. Twice he led the senior circuit in triples. He currently holds the Pirates record for stolen bases with 688.

Carey was one of the best examples of a "dirty shirt ballplayer." A scrappy fellow, he never feared throwing himself into the game—literally. This hard-nosed player earned a reputation for the kind of roughhouse play that sent many a second baseman to an early shower if he dared to block the base path when Carey was attempting a steal.

When scrappy Max Carey took the field, nobody would suspect that this rough-and-tumble player had once studied in a seminary to enter the Lutheran ministry.

In the 1925 World Series, despite suffering from agonizing injuries, Carey led all players with a .458 average, got 11 hits, including four doubles, stole three bases, and was hit by three pitched balls. Following the victorious Series, Carey was taken to the hospital, where he was discovered to have cracked ribs and a torn ligament on his right side. He remained hospitalized for a week.

Never timid about his records, Carey was his own best publicist for induction to the Hall of Fame—something he was able to enjoy 15 years before he died in 1976 at age 86 in Miami.

Lloyd "Little Poison" Waner (1967)

Joining the Pirates in 1927, only one year after his brother, Paul, Lloyd Waner grabbed a lot of attention in Pittsburgh and throughout the league when he batted .355 and scored a league-leading 133 runs.

Dubbed Little Poison by the opposition, Lloyd Waner constantly lived in the shadow of his older brother. Playing for Pittsburgh from 1927 to 1941 and from 1944 to 1945, Waner was a "slap hitter" who was able to punch the ball past infielders who had to play up close because of his speed.

As with his brother, Lloyd had a reputation for making contact with the baseball. In more than 8,000 trips to the plate, the younger Waner struck out only 173 times.

Waner's 18-year career was interrupted for two years when he temporarily traded his fielding glove for a welder's mitt, working in an airplane factory during World War II.

His career totals included 2,459 hits and a .316 lifetime average. He died in Oklahoma City in 1982 at the age of 76.

Roberto "the Great One" Clemente (1973)

Following the tragic death of Roberto Clemente in 1972, the Hall of Fame passed a new rule the next year waiving the five-year waiting period for anyone who died while on a major league roster. The first player to be inducted under this new provision was the Pirates' Roberto Clemente. Who better to demonstrate the sound thinking behind this decision than the Great One?

Roberto Clemente Walker (his given name) was the first Latin American baseball superstar, and he set the standard for playing right field. Local fans came to the ballpark just to see his riflelike arm and spectacular catches.

Relatively unnoticed by the national media until his spectacular performance in the 1971 World Series, Clemente played his entire career with Pittsburgh (1955–1972), during which he collected exactly 3,000 hits, 440 of which were doubles, 166 triples, and 240 home runs. He led the National League twice in hits and four times in batting average. With a .317 career average, Clemente was selected 12 times to play in the All-Star Game, won 12 Gold Gloves, and was voted the senior circuit's MVP in 1966, although many baseball experts agree that he should have won the honor at least two other times.

On New Year's Day 1973, Pirates fans were shocked to read of Clemente's untimely death resulting from an airplane crash off the shores of his native Puerto Rico. The 38-year-old All-Star and humanitarian had volunteered to accompany supplies being flown to earthquake victims in Nicaragua.

In conjunction with the 1994 All-Star Game at Three Rivers Stadium, the Pirates honored the Great One with a 12-foot statue that was moved to PNC Park, where it greets pedestrians who take the Roberto Clemente (formerly Sixth Street) Bridge to watch their Buccos play.

Ralph Kiner (1975)

When Ralph McPherran Kiner married tennis star Nancy Chaffee in October 1951, teenage girls in the Steel City wore black bobby socks as a sign of mourning. Not only had this tall, good-looking, sandy-haired home-run hitter become the heartthrob of young girls during his seven-plus years (1946–1953) with the Pirates, but he was the idol of *all* Pittsburghers.

Fans flocked to the ballpark at least 90 minutes prior to game time just to see Kiner take batting practice. They *ooohed* and *aaahed* as they watched many of his monstrous home runs still rising as they sailed over the scoreboard at Forbes Field. Although he played on mediocre squads, he gave Bucs fans a lot to be

In a rare photo opportunity prior to an exhibition game at Forbes Field between the Boston Red Sox and the Pirates in 1950, future Hall of Famers Ralph Kiner and Ted Williams prepare for a home-run-hitting contest (won by Kiner) prior to the game.

proud of as he held or tied for the league lead in home runs for an astonishing seven years in a row—a record that Babe Ruth, Hank Aaron, or Barry Bonds could not match. His 54 homers during the 1949 campaign still remain the most ever hit by a Pirate in one year.

Following his trade to the Cubs in 1953, Kiner acknowledged Pirates fans as "the greatest and most knowledgeable in the world."

A sore back forced Kiner to retire after only 10 seasons. Afterward he became a baseball executive with the Pacific Coast League San Diego Padres and in 1962 began a 45-plus-year stint behind the microphone with the New York Mets.

Twelve years after his induction to the Hall of Fame, Pittsburgh honored Kiner by retiring his No. 4. Later his name was added to the Ring of Fame at PNC Park. During a special pregame ceremony on Opening Day 2003, the team dedicated the special "Hitter's Hands" sculpture (a re-creation of his hands in bronze holding a bat) to Kiner in the left-field pavilion.

Regarding his future, Kiner sums it up in his newest book—*Baseball Forever*—"I always liked happy endings."

Joseph Floyd "Arky" Vaughan (1985)

The Pittsburgh Pirates were blessed with having on their rosters perhaps the two greatest shortstops in the history of Major League Baseball. The first was Honus Wagner; the second was a 5'10" native of Clifty, Arkansas, named Joseph Floyd Vaughan, better known as "Arky."

Vaughan, who spent 10 of his 14 years in the major leagues wearing a Pirates uniform (1932–1941), remains one of the most underrated shortstops ever to fill the position. He was constantly living and playing in the shadow of Wagner, who had retired 15 years earlier and became a coach with the team during Vaughan's sophomore season.

Not only was Vaughan a more-than-adequate fielder (a .951 fielding average as compared to Wagner's .940 average), but he also displayed surprising power for a shortstop. Three times he led the National League in triples and in runs scored. His .318 lifetime average included one year (1935) when he hit an incredible .385 to lead the league.

This nine-time All-Star was also a patient hitter, leading the senior circuit in walks three times.

His crowning moment came in the 1941 All-Star Game at Briggs Stadium in Detroit when he blasted two home runs. Unfortunately that feat was overshadowed when Boston's Ted Williams hit a homer to win it for the American League in the ninth.

Following his retirement from the game, Vaughan did not have much opportunity to take bows for his outstanding career. At the young age of 40, he and a friend were fishing when their boat capsized. Vaughan jumped into the lake in an attempt to save his friend, who could not swim. Both men drowned.

Willie "Pops" Stargell (1988)

At the memorial service for Wilver Dornel Stargell in 2001, former teammate and current broadcaster Steve Blass said, "I will always remember Willie Stargell, the 21-year-old stud. He ran like a deer, had a cannon for an arm, and he could make the ball disappear. Willie Stargell was, and always will be, a Bucco."

That, in a nutshell, summarized the career of, and reverence for, the greatest Pirates first baseman of all time.

MIXED EMOTIONS

"We find it ironic that on one of the greatest days for the Pirates franchise—the opening of PNC Park—it's also one of the saddest. We lost a great player and a friend, but we still believe that his presence will be felt at the ballpark today. You can go back to the entire history of the organization and not find a player who was more of a Pirate than Willie Stargell."

—Kevin McClatchy, managing general manager for the Pirates, on April 9, 2001, just two days following the dedication of the Willie Stargell statue at PNC park

Fans who saw him play still talk about how this burly left-hand-hitting slugger stood at home plate, twirling a 42-ounce bat in a windmill-like circle as if it were a twig. Opposing pitchers admitted that as he stood in the batter's box, he stared them squarely in the eye as if to say, "I own you."

Perhaps the best way to remember this gentle giant and first-ballot Hall of Famer is through the name given him by his teammates: Pops. It was a term of endearment for a man who was not only an imposing player—21 years in the big leagues (1962–1982) all with Pittsburgh, a career .282 average, 475 home runs, 2,232 hits, a seven-time All-Star, co-MVP, two-time National League home-run leader, six times a member of division-winning teams, twice on World Series champion squads—but also a leader, a motivator, and a role model for anyone who needed a personification of what was right.

The home-run blasts from this 6'2", 225-pound product of Earlsboro, Oklahoma, often surpassed by far anything fans had seen before. At Three Rivers Stadium in Pittsburgh, several seats high in the upper deck of the right-field stands contained stars marking the spots where his gargantuan blows landed. For a long time, he was the only man ever to hit a ball out of Dodger Stadium. Pirates fans who followed the team in the 1960s will recall that Stargell hit balls over the right-field roof at Forbes Field a record seven times.

In 1979, as the Pirates drove for the National League pennant and eventual victory over the Baltimore Orioles in the World Series, Stargell helped motivate his teammates by awarding so-called Stargell Stars that the players affixed to their caps. When a player was depressed, it was Stargell who shouted words of encouragement; when another was out of line for one reason or

BY THE NUMBERS

110—The most wins ever by a Pirates team (1909). And this was during a 154-game season.

another, he placed his giant arm around him and whispered some sage advice.

Following Stargell's retirement in 1982, he coached for the Pirates during the '85 season and followed his manager, Chuck Tanner, to Atlanta, where he coached and served the Braves' front office. He later returned to his rightful home turf, where he became a special assistant to Kevin McClatchy, the Pirates' then managing general partner.

On April 7, 2001—two days before PNC Park opened—the Pirates dedicated a 12-foot statute to their beloved Pops outside PNC Park's left-field gate on Federal Street. Suffering from kidney failure, the 61-year-old Stargell was too ill to attend the dedication ceremony. He died two days later in Wilmington, North Carolina.

Bill "Maz" Mazeroski (2001)

When Bill Mazeroski was inducted into the Hall of Fame in 2001, he proved that defensive skills were finally considered a vital part of the game of baseball.

In spite of the fact that Maz will probably be best remembered for his historic home run of October 13, 1960, that propelled the Pirates to a World Series championship over the heavily favored New York Yankees, he was never considered a power hitter. In 17 seasons (1956–1972)—all with the Pirates— the slick-fielding second baseman hit only 138 round-trippers in 2,163 games.

Named to seven All-Star teams and winner of the Gold Glove eight times, Mazeroski was dubbed "No Touch" by players around the league. When executing a double play, as he took the toss from the shortstop and fired to first base, he was so quick, it appeared as though he never handled the ball.

Endorsing this nickname was veteran sportswriter Bob Carroll, who once called Mazeroski "The da Vinci of the double play."

Hailing from nearby Wheeling, West Virginia, the popular Pirate ended his career as arguably the greatest fielding second baseman in history, holding the record for participating in the most double plays, with 1,706.

As if the gods of baseball were putting a final stamp of approval on all that William Stanley Mazeroski meant to the Pirates, at the last game ever played in Forbes Field on June 28, 1970, it was Maz's unassisted putout at second base that made the final out.

OTHER HALL OF FAMERS

Twenty-five other Hall of Fame inductees spent parts of their careers with the Pittsburgh Pirates. The images on their official plaques contain caps of other Major League Baseball clubs, but they were Pirates once:

Connie Mack (1937)   Branch Rickey (1967)
Jack Chesbro (1946)   Kiki Cuyler (1968)
Rube Waddell (1946)   Waite Hoyt (1969)
Frankie Frisch (1947)   Jake Beckley (1971)
Rabbit Maranville (1954)   Joe Kelley (1971)
Dazzy Vance (1955)   George Kelly (1973)
Joe Cronin (1956)   Billy Herman (1975)
Hank Greenberg (1956)   Al Lopez (1977)
Bill McKechnie (1962)   Chuck Klein (1980)
Burleigh Grimes (1964)   Vic Willis (1995)
Heinie Manush (1964)   Jim Bunning (1996)
Pud Galvin (1965)   Ned Hanlon (1996)
Casey Stengel (1966)

OTHER OUTSTANDING BUCS

Aside from the Pittsburgh Pirates who have gained notoriety as Hall of Famers, have had their numbers retired, or have had sculptures placed at PNC Park, others in the history of the organization have left a more-than-usual impact on the fans.

Someone might argue that these players were selected as a result of a personal preference as opposed to hard, cold statistics. That observation may be correct. If so, this author makes no apology. Baseball transcends statistics. It becomes part of the core of anyone who calls himself or herself a fan.

Trying, however, to be as objective as humanly possible, the author has chosen 20 players who have not otherwise been profiled in this book, yet who, for one reason or another, deserve to be called outstanding.

Mateo Rojas "Matty" Alou (1966–1970)

This 5'9" native of the Dominican Republic is living proof that a change of scenery can do a fellow a lot of good. When Mateo Rojas "Matty" Alou came to the Pirates as a center fielder in 1966, he was a .260 hitter with San Francisco. Bucs manager Harry Walker changed all that when he taught the left-hand-hitting Alou to slap the ball to the left side of the diamond instead of attempting to pull every pitch.

The results were astounding. Alou raised his average that year to .342, good enough to lead the National League. He would later appear in two All-Star Games as he continued to vie for batting crowns over the next four years.

Clarence "Ginger" Beaumont (1899–1906)

His real name was Clarence, but because of his dazzling blondish-red hair, his teammates nicknamed this burly Wisconsin native Ginger. In his eight years with the Pirates, Beaumont led the league three times in hits and in 1902 smacked a jaw-dropping .357.

Beaumont was a main ingredient (along with Honus Wagner, of course) of the 1903 team that played in the first World Series.

During the off-season, Beaumont worked on his Wisconsin dairy farm and became a highly successful businessman. Pirates owner Barney Dreyfuss suspected that because he was earning so much money as a farmer, Beaumont would not give 100 percent as a ballplayer. As a result, he traded his center fielder to Boston (then called the "Doves" in honor of Owner George Dovey) following the 1906 season.

Steve Blass (1964, 1966–1974)

His best year with the Bucs was in 1971, when he pitched a league-leading five shutouts, along with his 15–8 record and 2.85 ERA. As a bonus to him and to Pirates fans everywhere, Blass tossed a three-hit victory in Game 3 of the World Series and hurled a masterful four-hitter to win Game 7 against the Orioles.

The career of this pitcher with pinpoint control came to an end in 1974. For some reason known only to those far wiser than any of us, he was unable to find the strike zone.

Blass is now part of the Pirates broadcast team on radio and television and is active in the Pirates Alumni Association.

Bobby "Bobby Bo" Bonilla (1986–1991)

Possessing one of the most beautiful swings this side of Ted Williams, Bobby "Bobby Bo" Bonilla became one of the most valuable players on the Pirates during some turbulent, and ultimately disappointing, seasons in the late '80s and early '90s, when the Black and Gold came ever so close to winning it all.

As a third baseman, Bonilla was the "Jekyll and Hyde" of the hot corner. In 1988, for example, he led the league in assists and errors (32).

Bonilla is best remembered for his bat. The switch hitter pounded the ball with the best of them. He was only the seventh player to launch a drive into the upper deck at Three Rivers Stadium.

The six-time All Star (four with the Pirates) won the admiration of fans throughout the nation and once (1988) collected more votes for the midseason classic than did Mike Schmidt.

John "the Candy Man" Candelaria (1975–1985, 1993)

In Pittsburgh, if people mention the Candy Man, there's no doubt who they are talking about. Big (6'7", 232 pounds) John Candelaria turned heads when, in his third year with the Pirates (1977), he posted a 20–5 record (the first Pirates southpaw to record that many victories since Wilbur Cooper back in 1924); the

UNEXPECTED FIRE DRILL!

The final game of the 1972 National League Championship Series is one that Pirates fans, as well as players, would rather forget.

Going into the best-of-five series, the defending world champion Pirates, with the powerful lineup of Clemente, Stargell, Sanguillen, Oliver, Blass, Briles, and Giusti, were heavy favorites to take the series.

Leading 3–2 in the fifth and deciding game in the bottom of the ninth in Cincinnati, pitcher Dave Giusti gave up a tying home run to future Hall of Famer Johnny Bench. The Reds followed with two more singles. Bob Moose relieved Giusti and got two outs. With runners on first and third, Moose let go with a sharp slider that broke into the dirt and skipped by the catcher, Sanguillen, all the way to the backstop. George Foster, the runner on third, scored easily, and Cincinnati was headed to the World Series.

A sad, frustrated, and angry Pirates team flew back to Pittsburgh. Nobody spoke a word. Upon arrival at the airport, Steve Blass, Dave Giusti, and their wives shared a ride back to their homes. Again, everyone was silent, as they faced a long, cold winter.

When the car stopped for a traffic light, Blass suddenly yelled out: "Okay, everybody. Out for a fire drill. It's time to loosen up."

All four occupants leaped out of the vehicle. "We were so pissed off," recalled Blass, "we started to shout obscenities into the dark of the night. When we got done, we all felt better. We got back into the car and continued our drive home. We were now able to face the winter."

.800 winning percentage was tops in the National League that season.

Winning was rather usual for this lanky southpaw. He registered 177 wins during his 19 years in the major leagues. One year before his phenomenal '77 season, Candelaria became the first Pirate ever to pitch a no-hit, no-run game in Pittsburgh. It could not have come at a more opportune time. It was the 500th game played at Three Rivers Stadium and, as a plus, was aired on national television.

He led the 1979 world champion Bucs with 14 wins during the season and pitched shutout ball against Baltimore in Game 6 of the World Series.

Wilbur Cooper (1912–1924)

Okay, all you Pirates trivia buffs, answer this: What pitcher has won more games for the Bucs than any other? If you answered "Vernon Law," "ElRoy Face," or "Bob Friend," you would be close, but would not win any cigar. The answer is "Arley Wilbur Cooper."

Winning 202 games for Pittsburgh in 13 of his 15 big-league seasons, Cooper posted 20 or more wins in four seasons and 19 victories in two others. He led the league in 1921 with 22 wins and, during each of two campaigns, pitched an amazing 27 complete games.

Cooper's trademark pitch was a sharp-breaking sinker ball that made even the most astute hitters look foolish by swinging at balls in the dirt.

Matching his on-field talent was a temper that flared whenever a teammate misplayed a ball. Because of his unpopularity in the clubhouse, few tears were shed when the southpaw was shipped to the Cubs prior to the 1925 campaign.

Hazen Shirley "Kiki" Cuyler (1921–1927)

He was iron-willed and iron-fisted, which was a perfect match for fans in the Iron City.

It's true that when he was enshrined in Baseball's Hall of Fame, Hazen Shirley "Kiki" Cuyler was not introduced as a Pirate, rather as a Chicago Cub. At the same time, his image is on one of the banners hanging outside PNC Park. That might seem strange for someone who racked up only three and a half seasons as a starter for the Bucs. When we read his full story, the reason for this honor becomes clear.

The muscular 5'10", 180-pound outfielder did not see much playing time during his first three seasons but then enjoyed a bit more than four stellar years with Pittsburgh from 1924 to 1927 when he hit for an average of .325, led the league twice in runs scored, led once in triples, and was a threat each year to lead in stolen bases. During the 1925 World Series, he hit a double off Washington's Walter "Big Train" Johnson to win Game 7 of the fall classic.

Cuyler could have become one of the all-time Pirates greats in many of the offensive categories had it not been for a dispute with manager Donie Bush, who stubbornly benched him during the last half of the 1927 season for allegedly failing to hustle. Bush even kept him out of the entire World Series that year when the Pirates lost to the Yankees, four games to none.

Murry "the Thomas Edison of Baseball" Dickson (1949–1953)

He could have been regarded as a superstar, perhaps one of the greatest pitchers of all time, had it not been for one thing. Murry Dickson pitched for some of the worst teams in baseball when he was with the Pirates.

Called the Thomas Edison of baseball because he had so many pitches, Dickson had a 66–85 record as a Pirate. However, in 1951, he posted a 20–16 record for a team that finished the season with only 64 wins. That means he accounted for nearly one-third of the team's victories.

ElRoy Face (1953, 1955–1968)

While spending 15 of his 16 years in the show with the Pittsburgh Pirates, ElRoy Face redefined the art of relief pitching.

During his first three years in a Bucs uniform, Face compiled a modest record (23–28) as a starter and reliever. When Danny

A POTENT DIET

During one spring training, the 6'5", 230-pound massive slugger Dave Parker announced to a reporter that he was becoming a vegetarian.

Pirates pitcher John Candelaria read about it the next morning in the local newspaper and exclaimed, "What's he going to eat? Redwoods?"

Murtaugh came aboard as manager, the 5'8", 155-pounder became a relief specialist. It was here that Face discovered his home.

That became most apparent in 1959 when Face grabbed the baseball world's attention by notching 17 victories in a row. Ending the season with an 18–1 record and 10 saves, Face set standards few will ever challenge.

Pitcher ElRoy Face set the standard for modern-day relief pitchers.

One of the secrets of success for the three-time All-Star was a pitch he mastered known as the forkball—one that breaks sharply toward the ground just prior to reaching the plate.

He retired after the 1969 season with a total of 104 wins and 193 saves.

Bob Friend (1951–1965)

If there ever was an example of someone being in the wrong place at the wrong time, it was Bob Friend. This gifted right-handed pitcher from Lafayette, Indiana, spent 15 of his 16 major league years with the Pittsburgh Pirates at a time when, for most of those seasons, they were mired in the basement of the National League. Nonetheless, this three-time All-Star was the Pirates' ace during these dark days. In 1955, for instance, he led the last-place Bucs and the National League with a 2.83 ERA—the only time a pitcher for a cellar dweller was able to do this.

As the club got better, so did Friend's win-loss record. In 1958 he led the league with victories (22), and in the world championship season of 1960, he posted an 18–12 record and a 3.00 ERA.

Perhaps because he was able to succeed amid so much adversity, he felt qualified to enter the unforgiving arena of politics. Here he showed another dimension of skills as he was elected as an Allegheny County controller.

Dick Groat (1952, 1955–1962)

If God ever created a captain of a Major League Baseball team, he would use as a model Wilkinsburg's Dick Groat. This scrappy shortstop was not gifted with the raw talent of others in the big leagues, but he more than made up for it with an instinct for hitting, fielding, and motivating teammates.

This combination of ingredients was key to the Pirates capturing the World Series crown from the New York Yankees in 1960. His .325 batting average that year was good enough to win the league's title, as well as the MVP award.

The surprising fact is that this team captain nearly forsook baseball for another of his loves—basketball. An All-American at Duke, he played a season for the Fort Wayne Zollner Pistons (forerunners of the Detroit Pistons) of the National Basketball Association.

The Pirates and all of Pittsburgh were happy with his ultimate career choice.

Since 1979, Groat has been doing radio commentary for the University of Pittsburgh Panthers' basketball games.

Shortstop Dick Groat was a star in both baseball and basketball.

Frank Gustine (1939–1948)

When Leo Durocher allegedly coined the phrase "Nice guys finish last," he was not thinking of Frankie Gustine. This gentle second sacker (mostly) was a versatile infielder who could be counted on to play any position he was asked to fill. He even caught games in 1941 and 1945.

A three-time All-Star, Gustine became a local favorite with his aggressive play on the diamond and with the gentle rapport he established with the fans he happened to meet around Pittsburgh.

This .265 career hitter became even more popular after he opened his famous bar outside of Forbes Field that became a favorite hangout of fans and players alike.

Jason Kendall (1996–2004)

"Like father, like son." This adage applies to no one better than Fred Kendall, a 12-year major league veteran, and his son, Jason, who played nine memorable years with the Pittsburgh Pirates.

Like his father, Jason Kendall was a catcher, but not your average backstop by any means. Kendall was a solid hitter, leading the Bucs four seasons in batting average. In 1996, he was named *The Sporting News* Rookie of the Year. In addition, unlike most who field his position, he was fleet afoot, swiping 26 bases in 1998—a National League record for catchers.

On July 4, 1999, when Kendall was in the midst of what would probably have been his most productive season, he tripped over first base while attempting to beat out a bunt and fractured his leg. Showing the grit and determination that Pittsburghers were used to seeing in him, he returned to the lineup the next year with a sterling performance, leading the league in game appearances and at-bats for a catcher while hitting .320.

After being signed to a four-year, $40 million contract, Kendall, who was never known as a home-run hitter, had to be traded to Oakland for financial reasons in spite of the fact that he batted .319 during the 2004 season, his last as a Pittsburgh Pirate.

Ray Kremer (1924–1933)

Ray Kremer is a role model for persistence. After spending 10 long years in the minor leagues, he finally got the call to join the big leagues when he was 31 years old—an age when some of his colleagues seriously contemplated retirement from the game.

Kremer showed 'em all that he was still able to win when he ended his rookie season with an 18–10 record.

Not gifted with an overpowering fastball, Kremer was not a strikeout king but was able to notch two seasons in which he won 20 games and pitched well enough in two successful outings to enable the Pirates to defeat the Washington Senators in the 1925 World Series.

Twice, this native of Oakland, California, led the league in ERA, and he was the number one pitcher on the Pirates squad during seven of his 10 years with the team.

In spite of his late start in the show, Kremer won a total of 143 games, tying him for seventh place on the all-time list of the Pittsburgh Pirates.

Dale Long (1951, 1955–1957)

For eight days in 1956, there was never a better home-run hitter in the history of Major League Baseball than Dale Long.

Long, who spent less than three full years in a Pirates uniform, is still the subject of discussions among loyal fans that normally begin with: "Do you remember when Dale Long hit those home runs?"

From May 19 to 28, 1956, Long hit a home run in eight consecutive major league games—something never done before, and since equaled by only Don Mattingly (1987) and Ken Griffey Jr. (1993).

When Long smacked his eighth round-tripper before a packed house at Forbes Field, Pirates fans, who had little for which to be excited all year, rose to their feet and cheered with gusto. Long rounded the bases and went calmly into the dugout along the first-base line. The fans continued to cheer. Bob Skinner, the Bucs' next hitter, refused to step into the batter's box. The noise grew more intense. Finally, Long stepped from the dugout and took a bow.

RECORDS ARE MADE TO BE BROKEN—ANY WAY THEY CAN BE

On August 31, 1968, Pirates relief ace ElRoy Face was tied with Walter "Big Train" Johnson for the all-time record in pitching appearances—802—with one club.

Steve Blass, the starting pitcher that evening, retired the first hitter of the visiting Atlanta Braves when manager Larry Shepard called time and sent Blass to left field in a prearranged scenario. In from the bullpen came Face to pitch to only one batter—Felix Millan. Face and his forkball did well, as Millan grounded out weakly to short.

Shepard ordered Blass to return from the outfield, and Face walked to the dugout to a standing ovation from fans who showed their appreciation for the thrills he had given them over the years.

Blass continued to dominate the Braves until the last out of an 8–0 whitewash.

That accomplishment, however, did not make the next morning's headlines. Instead, it was the fact that, just a few hours before game time, Face had been sold to the Detroit Tigers, but Pirates management elected not to sign the final papers until Face broke the coveted record.

It was the first "curtain call" that anyone can remember a player taking.

Following an ovation that lasted a full 10 minutes, the game continued. The streak ended after that night, but the delicious memory of those days in May 1956 continue to be another part of the treasure owned by Pirates fans everywhere.

Dave "Cobra" Parker (1973–1983)

When 6'5", 230-pound rookie outfielder Dave Parker emerged from the Pirates dugout for the first time in mid-July 1973, Dal Maxvill, one of his teammates, said, "I don't know who this guy is, but I'm glad he's on our side."

Parker had as much raw talent as anyone who ever donned the black and gold of the Bucs. Voted seven times to the All-Star squad (four as a Pirate), Parker dazzled the National League with his dominant bat and equally powerful arm in right field. In the 1979 All-Star Game, Parker demonstrated his prowess to viewers of the nationally televised game when he threw out not just one, but two runners, attempting to take an extra base.

Cobra, as he was called, earned the MVP trophy in 1978, led his club in hitting for three consecutive years (1977–1979), and won two league batting championships (1977, 1978) and three Gold Gloves (1977, 1978, 1979). He also led the Pirates twice in home runs (25 in 1975, 30 in 1978).

Pirates management rewarded Parker for his stellar performance with a $7.9 million contract over five years. That blessing, unfortunately, became a curse. Pirates fans with a "steel-mill mentality" resented the fact that a man who played a "children's game" should receive so much money. Add to this mix some statements made by Parker to the press that were taken out of context, one fan became so irate, he threw a transistor radio battery at the slugger. Parker became a scapegoat for the Pirates' demise over the next few years and he signed on with Cincinnati following the '83 campaign.

After his retirement from baseball, Parker served as a hitting instructor for the Bucs in spring training.

Manny Sanguillen (1967, 1969–1976, 1978–1980)

Perhaps the only thing that outstripped this jovial Panamanian's talent as a catcher was his beaming smile. Today, Pirates fans gathering at PNC Park can meet this former Buc turned entrepreneur at his famous barbecue stand at the stadium.

Remembered in part as being one of the few players ever swapped for a manager (Chuck Tanner), Sanguillen was a versatile athlete. In addition to his .296 career batting average, he exhibited a solid defense and was a favorite backstop for Pirates pitchers.

He also provided a lot of excitement for the fans. Seldom content to walk, Sanguillen preferred to get on base through hitting—sometimes swatting pitches far out of the strike zone. That caused former Bucs GM Joe L. Brown to remark, "Whenever

Manny gets a walk, either it's an intentional pass or paralysis has set in."

Rip Sewell (1938–1949)

With a total of 133 wins, Truett Banks "Rip" Sewell became the winningest pitcher over the 1940s. The Pirates right-hander not only overpowered hitters with the usual assortment of fastballs and curves, but he also developed a pitch for which he would become most famous.

Instead of throwing directly at the catcher's mitt, Sewell confused batters and entertained fans by tossing the ball in a rainbow-like arc. Masterful opponents such as Stan Musial looked less than spectacular when swinging at this weird delivery that the press called the "blooper" or "eephus" pitch. The notice that the immortal Ted Williams hit two home runs in the 1946 All-Star Game was not nearly as newsworthy as the fact that the Boston slugger hit one of them off a Sewell blooper pitch.

Sewell is living proof of Yogi Berra's observation that "it's not over 'til it's over." In 1949, the Pirates named him a coach. During spring training, when it became obvious that the pitching staff was exceptionally thin, the Bucs added him to the active roster just prior to the start of the season. Sewell responded by pitching the Pirates to a 1–0 Opening Day victory over the Cubs in a game that took only one hour, 49 minutes to play.

Dick Stuart (1958–1962)

For five years as a Pittsburgh Pirate, Dick "Dr. Strangeglove" Stuart drew excitement each time he stepped to the plate. This muscular native of San Francisco had earned headlines when, in 1956, he clubbed 66 home runs for Lincoln, Nebraska, in the Class A Western League—a record that still stands.

Although he never led the majors in home runs (his highest 35 with the Pirates and 42 with the Red Sox), he occasionally put on some exhibitions of massive power when he became the first player ever to hit a ball over the iron gates in right-center field and over the batting cage that sat against the deepest part of center field at Forbes.

Stuart also became noted for his fielding—or lack thereof—and his teammates nicknamed him Dr. Strangeglove because of his erratic play.

Kent Tekulve (1974–1985)

With his sidearm/submarine delivery, the bespectacled, 6'4", 180-pound, rail-thin Kenton Charles "Teke" Tekulve led the National League in appearances in both 1978 and 1979. In the 1979 fall classic against Baltimore, he recorded three saves as he struck out 10 Orioles in just over nine innings.

And who can ever forget the picture of the Rubber Band Man as he was being mobbed by his teammates after registering the final out of the Series?

After spending the final four and a half years in the majors with the Phillies and Reds, Tekulve returned to live in the familiar haunts of the 'Burgh. Today he's president of the Pittsburgh Pirates Alumni Association and often appears at the annual PirateFests and winter carnivals.

PIRATES RETIRED NUMBERS

The Pirates organization has retired the numbers of 10 major leaguers in recognition of their excellence on the diamond. Their names and numbers appear on the Circle of Fame on the facing of the upper deck at PNC Park.

1—Billy Meyer, Manager (1954)
4—Ralph Kiner, OF (1987)
8—Willie Stargell, 1B/OF (1982)
9—Bill Mazeroski, 2B (1987)
11—Paul Waner, OF (2007)
20—Pie Traynor, 3B (1972)
21—Roberto Clemente, OF (1973)
33—Honus Wagner, Coach (Note: Wagner never wore a uniform number as a player) (1952)
40—Danny Murtaugh, 2B/Manager (1977)
42—Jackie Robinson (retired by all clubs) (1997)

DADDY DEAREST

When the average fan follows a Major League Baseball team, he or she can often cite batting averages, which hitter is hot and which is not, and which pitcher should be on the mound that evening. Not everyone, however, can rattle off the names of the owner, general manager, or even the field manager.

In reality, the formation of any Pirates squad becomes the responsibility of the people holding all three of these titles. They are commissioned to give to Buccos fans the best combination of ingredients to produce a competitive team each season. This challenge is greatly enhanced when we realize that the financial resources available to keep players who become free agents after their sixth years of major league service are substantially less than those of metropolitan areas such as New York, Chicago, or Los Angeles.

Considering the revenue disparity between the Pirates and "big-market" teams, it's to the credit of Pirates owners and management that our Buccos have been able to survive in an industry dominated by big dollars.

THE OWNERS

Most of us have never seen them. Some may not be able to tell you their names. Yet they're the most powerful people in this history of the Pittsburgh Pirates. They're the team owners.

THOU SHALT NOT...

Barney Dreyfuss, owner of the Bucs from 1900 to 1932, was a fierce competitor whose biography resembled the script of a Damon Runyon story. Immigrating to the United States from Germany at age 17, he personified the American dream by working his way up the ladder of success, in spite of prejudices during this era against Germans and Jews.

A conservative, often stubborn businessman, Dreyfuss neither drank alcohol nor touched tobacco, and he had little to do with those who did. Once, a baseball enthusiast encouraged him to sign a 6'1" right-hand, hard-throwing pitcher from Humboldt, Kansas, named Walter Johnson. Dreyfuss refused because the man who made the recommendation was a cigar salesman.

In another classic blunder, Dreyfuss and the Pirates had an opportunity to land a flashy outfielder, Tris Speaker. That offer went by the wayside once Dreyfuss learned that the player was a smoker.

These people are the ones ultimately responsible for the team's location, for the ballpark, for the players, and for everything else associated with the club.

As with managers and general managers, owners have different philosophies about how to build a successful franchise. The Yankees' George Steinbrenner, for example, believes that you can scour the free-agency market and purchase a winning team. The late Bill Veeck promoted special events and outrageous door prizes in an attempt to draw fans to see his Cleveland Indians, St. Louis Browns, and Chicago White Sox.

Pittsburgh Pirates owners had to adopt different approaches. Their teams were not blessed with the large fan base of New York City or Chicago. Also, they were, by comparison, strapped for funds.

When the Pirates entered the big-league scene, the influx of money for any team depended solely on the amount of cash generated by fans who walked through the turnstiles. Today the intertwining of multimillion-dollar television contracts, corporate sponsorships, and sophisticated luxury boxes increase the number of revenue sources and create an even greater challenge for a small-market, low-revenue team such as the Pirates to compete for talent in the blizzard of free agency with teams in larger metropolitan areas.

Pirates fans, therefore, owe a huge debt of gratitude to those who have risked millions of dollars by purchasing the Pittsburgh Pirates baseball club and did whatever it took to keep our Bucs in the Steel City.

William A. Nimick (1887–1891)

The Pittsburgh club (called the "Alleghenies" until 1891) was part of the American Association (A.A.) in 1886. The A.A. was, for all practical purposes, a minor league as compared to the more powerful National League.

When the Kansas City Cowboys were ousted from the National League (primarily because of the travel time necessary for visiting teams), William Nimick, owner of the Pittsburgh franchise, took a gamble, resigned from the American Association, and applied for admission to the "real" major league. His gamble paid off, and Pittsburgh, a callow city of only 200,000 citizens, was now part of the 12-team National League.

Nimick's greatest test as an owner came in 1890 with the formation of the renegade Players League. The competitive league lasted only one year but left a trail of bitterness and lack of trust between players and owners.

Eventually Nimick turned over operations to one of his employees, J. Palmer O'Neill. However, O'Neill was not content with remaining in the background. He insisted on dictating whom Pirates manager Ned Hanlon should play in various situations.

Egos clashed. Tempers flared. Tired of all the fighting, a disgusted Nimick sold the team in 1891.

William Kerr and Phil Auten (1892–1899)

Two men teamed as owners of the club. One was William "Captain" Kerr, a top executive with Arbuckle Coffee and a micromanager. The other, Philip Auten, preferred to remain a silent partner.

Following eight years of playing fairly good ball when Pittsburgh notched six seasons with records of .500 or better, the National League voted to cut back from 12 teams to eight.

Following two ho-hum seasons, Kerr saw an opportunity to make a substantial profit. He came close to selling the Pittsburgh club before Barney Dreyfuss, owner of the now-defunct Louisville Colonels, offered to acquire 50 percent of the Pirates following the 1899 season through an off-beat agreement that included his bringing some top-notch players to Pittsburgh. Kerr accepted Dreyfuss's offer.

The merger of the Colonels and the Pirates allowed Pittsburgh to field dazzling players such as Honus Wagner. Over the next two years, the club won league championships. Kerr, however, felt that he was not given enough credit for his contributions and sold out to Dreyfuss.

Barney Dreyfuss (1900–1932)

When Barney Dreyfuss, a 34-year-old, 5'7" German Jewish immigrant, brought from Louisville a group of quality players, including Honus Wagner, Claude Ritchey, Tommy Leach, Charley Zimmer, and Deacon Phillippe, he all but guaranteed

Entrepreneur and businessman Barney Dreyfuss was instrumental in developing the Pirates during their early years.

that the Pittsburgh baseball club would be the powerhouse of the National League.

In addition to fielding solid players, Dreyfuss appointed a zealous manager in the person of Fred "Cap" Clarke, who guided the club to World Series appearances in 1903 and 1909.

Dreyfuss was also a young visionary with hopes and dreams. He invested more than $1 million into the construction of a state-of-the-art ballpark named Forbes Field. The city of Pittsburgh responded with years of record attendance for some outstanding teams.

With his passing in 1932, Dreyfuss left an envied legacy as measured by length of service (32 years), National League pennants (six), and World Series championships (two).

Assuming the title of owner after the death of Dreyfuss was his son-in-law, Bill "Bensy" Benswanger.

Bill Benswanger (1932–1946)

Bill Benswanger was not a baseball man. He was an insurance executive. When his father-in-law died, Benswanger reluctantly agreed to take the team.

He became an apt student of the game. He used his business savvy to help the club endure the negative effects caused by the Great Depression and the drafting of players for military service in World War II. He also initiated programs that proved beneficial. Two of the more popular traditions he established were Kids' Day, during which youngsters 12 years old and younger were allowed to watch the games free from the right-field stands, and Ladies' Day, when, for 50¢, a woman could purchase a reserve seat for Thursday afternoon games. The extra cash resulting from concession sales justified these promotions. A long-term bonus came with the addition of loyal fans.

In 1946 Benswanger sold the club for $2.5 million to a group headed by John Galbreath and Frank McKinney.

The Galbreath Group (1946–1985)

Baseball clubs were becoming more expensive to buy. Team ownership shifted from individuals or families to groups of investors who were required to pool their funds to make things work. The Galbreath Group became one of the first syndicates to do just that.

A realtor from Columbus, Ohio, and owner of the Darby Dan Farms in Ocala, Florida, John Galbreath convinced others to join him in purchasing the Pirates. His roster of investors included an Indianapolis banker (Frank McKinney), a Pittsburgh attorney (Tom Johnson) and a pretty good baritone from Hollywood (Harry Lillis "Bing" Crosby).

At first, the new owners' decisions about players and managers were not always the best. Consequently, the Pirates languished at or near the bottom of the league for the most part. It took the Galbreath Group nearly 15 years to find the right combination of raw talent and judicious leadership. In 1960, general

During spring training in 1948, one of the Pirates owners—crooner Bing Crosby— had a chance to offer some advice to new manager Billy Meyer.

manager Joe L. Brown, field manager Danny Murtaugh, and talented players such as Bill Mazeroski, Vernon Law, and Roberto Clemente gave the fans of Pittsburgh something they hadn't seen since 1925—a World Series championship.

Forbes Field, with all of its historic significance, had to be replaced. In its stead, the owners built Three Rivers Stadium, which was received with mixed reviews. In 1980, when it was only 10 years old, the multipurpose stadium already showed signs of deterioration, as did attendance. Although they became the proud owners of the World Series champs of 1971 and 1979, the Galbreath Group enjoyed few triumphs for which they could pop champagne corks.

Before they sold the club in 1985, the Galbreath Group won six Eastern Division titles, three National League pennants, and three world championships.

Pittsburgh Associates (1985–1996)

In 1985, the future of the Pirates in Pittsburgh looked as gloomy as the Allegheny County skies prior to a snowstorm. Drug scandals, player strikes, gargantuan salaries, and rising ticket prices made it increasingly difficult for the city with a "steel-mill mentality" to remain excited about its baseball club.

When the Galbreath Group actively investigated the potential of moving the team to New Orleans, Pittsburgh mayor Richard Caliguiri did everything except don a Superman costume to keep the Buccos in town. Using a combination of charisma and old-fashioned arm-twisting, he convinced 13 corporations to contribute $2 million each. He also got the city to cough up another $25 million through a bond issue to match the asking price of $51 million for the club.

The 12 years of ownership by Pittsburgh Associates were marked by a mixed bag of news. Three Eastern Division titles were about the only rewards for the investors. On the downside were bold headlines about internal fights, struggles for power, and the untimely death of Mayor Caliguiri.

Free agency opened the door for some of the Pirates' superstars—Barry Bonds, John Smiley, Bobby Bonilla, and Doug

Drabek—to trade uniforms, as they demanded higher salaries in a sport that was now awash in money—at least in some markets.

By 1996, the sky once again looked dark for the team's prospects in Pittsburgh. Fortunately for everyone, out of the west appeared a modern version of a knight in shining armor.

Kevin McClatchy/Robert Nutting (1996–Present)

The new hero in town during that uncertain period of Pittsburgh's history was 33-year-old Kevin McClatchy, heir to a famous Sacramento-based newspaper fortune, who purchased the Pirates for $90 million.

Shortly after arriving in Pittsburgh, McClatchy gave two commitments: to build a new, baseball-only park and to keep the Pirates in the Steel City. Both promises renewed baseball excitement around the 'Burgh.

With limited funds, McClatchy had to spend wisely. Although he authorized some hefty contracts for players such as Jason Kendall and Brian Giles, the outpouring of dollars was small compared to other franchises. Major investments in the club by G. Ogden Nutting, a Wheeling, West Virginia, newspaper magnate, and former owner Tom Johnson helped ease the crunch. Nonetheless, monies spent on salaries in Pittsburgh ranked at or near the bottom of Major League Baseball.

McClatchy's crowning achievement has to be the creation of PNC Park—the most beautiful ballpark in America. It provided a perfect setting for a game, and one of which Pittsburgh fans everywhere have the right to be mighty proud.

A subtle restructuring of the Pirates organization occurred on January 13, 2007, when both McClatchy and 44-year-old Robert M. "Bob" Nutting (Ogden's eldest son) held a joint news conference announcing that Nutting was assuming the role as principal owner, while McClatchy would remain chief executive officer and retain authority on day-to-day operations. Later McClatchy announced he would remain as an owner but would step down as CEO following the 2007 season.

KEVIN McCLATCHY'S BILL OF RIGHTS

When 33-year-old Kevin McClatchy purchased the Pittsburgh Pirates in 1996, he faced an up-hill battle to win the confidence of the fans and of the media.

Baseball was still in a funk resulting from a strike by the players just two years prior and, because the Bucs played in a small-market venue, rumors circulated that the team might be forced to move to a larger, more lucrative city.

McClatchy could do nothing about the ill feelings due to the strike; he could, however, put to rest any anxiety about a possible move out of town.

To emphasize his intentions, he penned something he called *Fans' Bill of Rights* that read:

1. We pledge to follow a proven model to rebuild this franchise into a championship team.
2. We pledge to keep baseball affordable for everyone in Pittsburgh, especially families.
3. We pledge to work to secure a public-private financing package to build a new baseball-only ballpark in Pittsburgh.
4. We pledge to make baseball fun in Pittsburgh.
5. We pledge to work with area youth organizations to encourage baseball enthusiasm.
6. We pledge to work with local officials to explore new transportation plans so that everyone can come to see the Pirates.
7. We pledge to work with the Pittsburgh business community to make Pirates baseball a greater economic plus for the region.
8. We pledge to talk Pirates baseball as often as we can to anyone who will listen.
9. We pledge that we will do anything we can to cultivate your trust and support of the Pirates.
10. We pledge that we will not move the Pirates from Pittsburgh.

Nutting had kept a low profile during the previous 11 years when McClatchy served as managing general partner. At the news conference, the media and fans met someone who could be a movie producer's dream. The tall, athletic graduate of Williams College is a rugged outdoorsman. He is a fly fisherman, skier, hunter, trap shooter, and avid conservationist. In addition, he has both private and commercial pilot's licenses and flies his twin-engine Beechcraft Baron across the country for business and pleasure. Keenly aware of the disappointments that Pirates management and fans experienced during 15 consecutive years of losing seasons, Nutting believes that the team has a nucleus of talented young players that will serve as a solid base for winning teams in the future.

THE GENERAL MANAGERS

Prior to 1946, when John Galbreath and Frank McKinney assumed responsibilities for the day-to-day operations of the Pittsburgh baseball club, the owners determined which players would be on the team roster. Neither Galbreath nor McKinney, however, was a baseball expert; both were businessmen. Fortunately for Pirates fans, they understood their limitations and elected to hire a general manager—someone with expertise to make baseball personnel decisions.

Since then, nine general managers have contributed to the fortunes, or misfortunes, of the club. Sometimes their trades have been strokes of genius; at others, they left astute fans scratching their heads in wonder.

For any general manager to be deemed a success, he must excel in number one of what we might call psychologist Abraham Maslow's Hierarchy of Baseball Needs: assemble pennant-winning teams without spending a pile of money.

With 20/20 hindsight, it's much easier for us to determine what moves Pirates GMs should or should not have made. As a result, opinions about general managers continue to be subjects for heated debate.

H. Roy Hamey (1946–1950)

The first person to have the title "Pirates General Manager" painted on his office door was H. Roy Hamey, the former president of the minor league American Association.

BE SURE TO READ THE FINE PRINT

In his popular book *Baseball Forever,* Ralph Kiner recalls the story of general manager Roy Hamey, who was able to convince Detroit Tigers superstar Hank Greenberg to postpone his retirement and to play for the 1947 Pittsburgh Pirates.

The terms of the contract included a salary of $100,000 (making him the first player in the National League ever to reach that plateau) and a yearling from the Darby Dan Farm of John Galbreath, a minority owner of the Pirates. That was the clincher. Greenberg's wife—Caral Gimbel (of the Gimbel's Department Store family)—was a passionate equestrian. Also, with the added value of the racehorse, Greenberg would surpass Joe DiMaggio and Ted Williams as baseball's highest-paid player.

Something (or some thoroughbred) must have fallen through the cracks, however. Greenberg never saw the horse.

Hamey wasted little time to make headlines. In 1947, he brought to the club future Hall of Famer Hank Greenberg from the Detroit Tigers for a reported $75,000. That purchase enabled the Pirates to have in its lineup the two 1946 home-run champions—Greenberg with 44 homers, and Ralph Kiner, who had hit 23.

To help increase the power output, Hamey and the owners shortened the left-field fence (365 feet away from home plate) by 30 feet when they installed bullpens in left and left-center fields. The new structure was baptized "Greenberg Gardens." Greenberg, however, would be limited that season by an ailing back and hit only 25 home runs, while slugger Kiner benefited from Greenberg's tutelage and smacked 51.

Despite the fact that the excitement generated by Kiner brought record crowds to Forbes Field, the Bucs could only tie for last place, and Greenberg retired as a player at the season's end.

One of the reasons for the club's poor showing in '47 was that prior to the season, Hamey opted to trade third baseman Bob Elliott to the Boston Braves for player/manager Billy Herman.

Elliott would go on to win the MVP award that year, while Herman was limited by a sore arm to playing in only 15 games. Things appeared to turn around the next year after Hamey acquired Bob Chesnes to beef up the pitching staff, plus Stan Rojek and Danny Murtaugh to solidify the middle infield. They helped the Bucs make a genuine run for the pennant, finishing in fourth place, just two games behind the second-place St. Louis Cardinals. The next two years resulted in losing seasons. Hamey resigned as GM in November 1950.

Branch Rickey (1951–1955)

Wesley Branch Rickey will be best remembered as the man who, while with the Brooklyn Dodgers, helped orchestrate the breaking of the color barrier in Major League Baseball. Prior to that historic decision, he developed for the St. Louis Cardinals a new concept called a "farm system," in which young talent was schooled in the finer points of the game. The system proved to be successful, and Rickey became infected with the notion that this system could work anytime with any team.

When the Pirates brought this 69-year-old legend into the fold in 1951, Rickey assumed bold leadership, as would a monarch who believed in the divine right of kings. He sought to turn around the Pirates franchise by developing young talent in the minor leagues. These prospects failed to blossom as predicted, and the Pirates faithful became increasingly angry at the lack of a pennant contender.

The fans, media, and management grew more irritated in 1952 when Rickey initiated absurd trades and went so far as to dictate to the field manager who should play. The disastrous 112-game losing season (in a campaign that lasted only 154 games) of the so-called Rickey Dinks became his ball and chain. Even his most loyal disciples clamored for drastic measures.

That change came the next year when Rickey swapped Pittsburgh idol Ralph Kiner in a 10-player trade with the Chicago Cubs. The deal produced no positive change, as the Pirates again finished in last place, a whopping 55 games behind the league-leading Brooklyn Dodgers.

After he announced his retirement as general manager in 1955, Rickey remained with Pittsburgh for a few years as a vice president.

Joe L. Brown (1956–1976, 1985)

He was the son of the world-famous comedian Joe E. Brown, but the third general manager of the Pirates saw nothing funny about the team's plight when he assumed his new role in '56.

Brown had an extensive baseball background, first as a player whose career was cut short by a broken arm, then in a variety of positions with minor league franchises that included selling tickets, driving team buses, and writing press releases, as well as filling several front-office jobs.

Pirates executives often show their latent ambitions of playing in the big leagues, as general manager Joe L. Brown (playing the role of catcher) and manager Bobby Bragan (at bat) demonstrate here in 1956.

His value in team-building became apparent when, during his first year with the Bucs, he landed players such as Bill Virdon. In 1958, following a second-place finish by the Pirates, Brown was named *The Sporting News* Executive of the Year.

His ability to make deals paid off with the unforgettable victory by the Bucs over the highly favored New York Yankees in the 1960 World Series. His skill in judging players helped bring Eastern Division crowns to Pittsburgh in 1970, 1971, 1972, 1974, and 1975, plus a world championship in 1971.

Following his retirement in 1976, the Pirates recalled Brown in 1985 to revamp a struggling team. He did just that, and the new personnel paved the way for the team's return to glory a few years later.

Harding Peterson (1976–1985)

Galbreath selected as his new GM another wannabe big-league baseball player, former catcher Harding "Pete" Peterson, who served as the Pirates' farm director.

Following in the footsteps of the popular Joe L. Brown, Peterson was also adept at making bold moves, including swapping All-Star catcher Manny Sanguillen and some cash to Oakland for manager Chuck Tanner.

Other gutsy moves brought high-caliber players such as Phil Garner, Bill Madlock, Tim Foli, Bert Blyleven, and John Milner. Together they would form the nucleus of the team known affectionately as the Fam-A-Lee that went on to defeat the Baltimore Orioles in the 1979 World Series.

Trades over the next few years proved to be less successful, and with the demise of the team came the loss of confidence in Peterson. Finally, in May 1985 Galbreath fired his GM.

Syd Thrift (1985–1988)

A new Pirates ownership group, known as Pittsburgh Associates, arrived on the scene with a pledge to keep the team in Pittsburgh and turn the last-place Pirates into a pennant contender. Named as general manager was Virginia native Syd Thrift, who invented the "baseball academy" while an executive with the Kansas City Royals.

General manager Syd Thrift reviews strategy with manager Jim Leyland in 1987.

Thomas Jefferson once said, "If you want to create enemies, start making changes." Changes and enemies are exactly what Thrift made when he replaced the popular Chuck Tanner as manager with the relatively unknown Jim Leyland. Another last-place finish the next year did not endear Thrift to the fans.

Undaunted, the feisty GM brought over pitcher Doug Drabek and slugger Bobby Bonilla. Later he acquired Andy Van Slyke, Mike LaValliere, and Mike Dunne. The Pirates showed solid improvement in 1987 and played close to .500 ball.

Thrift, however, wanted more control of the club, and that did not sit well with Pirates president Malcolm "Mac" Prine. In a "shootout" at a board meeting, Thrift won. Prine resigned.

A second-place finish in 1988 only fueled Thrift's desire for more control. Several of his quotes published in the *Pittsburgh Post-Gazette* led some readers to conclude that he was taking full credit for the team's success, further irritating others in management. In a new confrontation before the board with the team president, Carl Barger, Thrift's luck ran out, and he was summarily dismissed.

Larry Doughty (1988–1992)

One would think that a general manager for a National League club who molded three Eastern Division championships in a five-year period would be heralded as a success. Not so with Larry Doughty, who was terminated in 1992.

Doughty and his assistant, Cam Bonifay, had added some key players to the roster, including Don Slaught, Jay Bell, and Bill Landrum. On the flip side, he allowed the Bucs' top outfield prospect, Wes Chamberlain, to slip through his fingers on waivers, with the mistaken notion that he could pull him back. He also alienated the fan-favorite Bobby Bonilla through some uncomplimentary remarks.

Doughty is a classic victim of the age-old question "What have you done for me lately?"

Ted Simmons (1992–1993)

New Pirates president Mark Sauer came to Pittsburgh from the front office of the St. Louis Cardinals. When the vacancy appeared for the position of Pirates general manager, Sauer called for former All-Star Cardinals catcher Ted Simmons over Cam Bonifay, whom most considered to be Doughty's natural successor.

The task given to Simmons was to tear apart the roster and rebuild the team. To the surprise of everyone close to the organization, the Pirates played better than they knew how. With fine performances by newcomers Danny Jackson and consistent good play from Doug Drabek and Barry Bonds, the Bucs won the Eastern Division but were defeated in the National League Championship Series with a painful loss to the Atlanta Braves in the last inning of Game 7.

We'll never know just how far this energetic former Cardinal could have taken the Bucs. Simmons, a heavy smoker, suffered a heart attack while seated behind his desk in the Pirates office. He recovered following emergency surgery, but realized that, if he hoped to live a normal life, he would have to seek a less stressful line of work. Just 11 days following his attack, he resigned.

Cam Bonifay (1993–2001)

Cam Bonifay certainly did not want to inherit the general manager's job as a result of a heart attack by his predecessor, but that's precisely how he attained that position.

Perhaps no general manager ever entered the scene with such obvious success. With a payroll cut to approximately $9 million, he and his Pirates became viable contenders for the Central Division (the Bucs' new bracket as of 1994) crown by 1997. *The Sporting News* named Bonifay Executive of the Year and labeled the Pirates front office the Organization of the Year.

Some productive trades brought to the Pirates players such as Jason Schmidt, Jon Lieber, Craig Wilson, Kevin Young, and, perhaps the most noteworthy, slugger Brian Giles.

Ironically, when he had more money available, Bonifay's luck turned sour. He signed free agents who, on the surface, looked promising but ended up being unproductive. One of the most notable was infielder Pat Meares, who suffered what was thought to be a minor finger injury that eventually ended his career. Another was Derek Bell, who felt unappreciated when he discovered during the opening weeks of spring training he would have to vie for an outfield position and announced to the press that he was prepared to engage in an "operation shutdown."

That was all she wrote for Bonifay, who was fired in the middle of the 2001 season.

Dave Littlefield (2001–2007)

From the first day he took the job, Dave Littlefield was under pressure to create a competitive team despite other clubs being able to find payrolls two, three, even four times the budget allotted him. That reality, in concise terms, was the seemingly impossible challenge facing this quiet graduate of the University of Massachusetts.

Financial restrictions demanded that Littlefield unload high-dollar players. Fans, however, feel that he did not get enough in return for the likes of Jeff Suppan, Jason Schmidt, Jason Kendall,

Sean Casey, Aramis Ramirez, Chris Young, or Kenny Lofton. On the positive side, Littlefield was able to land the 2004 National League Rookie of the Year, Jason Bay, and 2006 National League batting champion, Freddy Sanchez.

On September 7, 2007, Littlefield was relieved of his duties following a combined 442–581 record during his tenure. He was replaced by Neal Huntington.

BEST AND WORST MOVES BY GENERAL MANAGERS

Quite possibly the most difficult role to fill in any major league front office is that of the general manager. That person must have the wisdom of Solomon and the foresight of a seer in order to decide which player will serve the team best over the coming years. The general manager must also be willing to swap an established player who has had his best years and is on the downside of his career for a young, untested prospect.

With 20/20 hindsight, we can easily judge these actions. At the moments of truth, however, the general manager can listen to all the advice offered him by the scouts, front-office staff, media, and fans. In the end, it is a one-person decision.

Sometimes, these judgments are reached with the help of computers and statistics. On other occasions, they result from a gut feeling.

Following are some remarkably great, and some not-so-great, moves by Pirates general managers.

Good Moves

1899: Getting Honus Wagner, Fred Clarke, Rube Waddell, and 11 other players from Louisville for Jack Chesbro, three other players, and $25,000. When the Louisville team disbanded one year later, Chesbro returned to the Pirates. Wagner, of course, was the major player in the deal. As one of the original five players inducted into the Hall of Fame, he is cited by many baseball experts even today as the greatest shortstop ever to play the game.

1948: Getting Danny Murtaugh and Johnny Hopp from the Boston Braves for Bill Salkeld, Al Lyons, and Jim Russell. Murtaugh would emerge as a premier second baseman and four-time Pirates manager.

1952: Getting Dick Groat from the NBA. This collegiate basketball All-Star from Duke University played for the Fort Wayne Zollner Pistons. The Pirates persuaded him to play baseball. This he did exceptionally well, winning the MVP award in 1960 when he was the National League batting champion and captain of the world champion Pirates. The five-time All-Star (three with Pittsburgh) is still a favorite among his neighbors in the Pittsburgh area.

1954: "Stealing" Roberto Clemente from the Dodgers farm system as Brooklyn attempted to hide him from other clubs. Clemente would become a 12-time All-Star, 12-time Gold Glove winner, four-time batting champion, winner of the MVP award (1966), World Series MVP, collector of 3,000 hits, and a Hall of Fame inductee.

1959: Getting Harvey Haddix, Don Hoak, and Smoky Burgess from Cincinnati for Frank Thomas, Whammy Douglas, Jim Pendleton, and John Powers. Haddix, Hoak, and Burgess would lead the Bucs to their amazing 1960 World Series crown. And who could ever forget that 12-inning perfect game tossed by Haddix in 1959?

1979: Getting Bill Madlock, Dave Roberts, and Lenny Randle from the San Francisco Giants for Eddie Whitson, Al Holland, and Fred Breining. Madlock, especially, was a key to turning the '79 season around and for the eventual victory of the Pirates over the highly favored Orioles in the 1979 World Series.

1987: Getting Andy Van Slyke, Mike "Spanky" LaValliere, and Mike Dunne from St. Louis for Tony Pena. Van Slyke and LaValliere would be fixtures who would help form the nucleus of the 1990–1992 National League Eastern Division champions.

1989: Getting Jay Bell from the Cleveland Indians for Felix Fermin and Denny Gonzalez. Bell would become a fixture at shortstop for eight years and would be chosen twice for a place on the National League All-Star team.

1998: Getting Brian Giles from Cleveland for Ricardo Rincon. Giles, a two-time All-Star, was a fan favorite who was the Bucs' only consistent power threat during his five years (1999–2003) with the team.

2003: Getting Jason Bay from the San Diego Padres for the aforementioned Brian Giles. To trade the most popular Pirate for a relative unknown was not only a courageous decision, but one that had to be taken if for no other reason than salary constraints. Bay, however, became Pittsburgh's most pleasant surprise in years. Winning the Rookie of the Year Award in '04 (the first ever for a Buc), this Canadian-born athlete has become a perennial All-Star who is also an outstanding role model for youngsters.

Bad Moves

1901: Selling Rube Waddell, who led the league in strikeouts and posted a 2.37 ERA, to the Chicago Cubs. He would go on to become the ace of the Philadelphia Athletics. As a strikeout king, he would lead the league six times in his 13-year career. He was also inducted into the Hall of Fame.

1915: Selling Dazzy Vance, who pitched only one game for the Bucs, to the New York Yankees. Vance was another Hall of Famer who was let go by the Pirates. Spending most of his 16-year career with the Brooklyn Dodgers, he would win a total of 197 games.

1918: Trading Burleigh Grimes and two players to Brooklyn for Casey Stengel and George Cutshaw. Grimes would post a 19–9 record that year and win 270 games over a 19-year career, earning Hall of Fame honors in 1964. Meanwhile, Cutshaw played second base for four years with the Bucs, and Stengel would appear as an outfielder in only 124 games over two seasons.

1928: Trading Kiki Cuyler to the Chicago Cubs for Sparky Adams and Pete Scott because of a dispute with Pirates manager Donie Bush. Cuyler would play for 11 more years and compile a .321 career batting average. He was elected to the Hall of Fame in 1968 and inducted as a Cub.

1938: Passing on a southpaw pitcher from nearby Donora, Pennsylvania, at tryout camp. His name was Stan Musial. He would compile a .331 batting average over 22 years in the big leagues. This Hall of Famer would become a seven-time batting champion, earn three MVPs, and be voted to the All-Star team a remarkable 20 times.

1946: Swapping Bob Elliott and Hank Camelli to the Boston Braves for Billy Herman, Elmer Singleton, Stan Wentzel, and Whitey Wietelmann. Elliott, the key player in the swap, would have a spectacular year in '47, winning the National League MVP award. Herman was brought in as a player/manager for the Bucs, but lasted only one year.

1948: Getting Vic Lombardi, Hal Gregg, and Dixie Walker from the Brooklyn Dodgers for Preacher Roe, Billy Cox, and Gene Mauch. Roe would become a four-time All-Star and post a 22–3 record in 1951. Cox was the Dodgers' rock at third base for seven years.

1952: Getting Cal Abrams, Gail Henley, and Joe Rossi from the Cincinnati Reds for Gus Bell, who would go on to capture four All-Star appearances and become a mainstay in the Reds' organization for nine seasons.

1957: Getting Don Gross from Cincinnati for Bob Purkey, who would star for the Reds, winning three selections to the All-Star team and, in 1962, leading the league in winning percentage with a 23–5 record.

1984: Getting George Hendrick from the St. Louis Cardinals for John Tudor and Brian Harper. The next year Tudor won 21 games and posted a 1.93 ERA. Harper won acclaim later with the world champion Minnesota Twins (1991).

2000: Signing Derek Bell, who would play in only 46 games in 2001 and "amass" a .173 batting average. During spring training the next year, he threatened to have an "operation shutdown" because he was told he had to compete for the role as starting right fielder. He was released shortly thereafter.

2001: Getting Armando Rios and Ryan Vogelsong from the Giants for Jason Schmidt and John Vander Wal. Schmidt would become one of the premier hurlers in the National League.

BY THE NUMBERS

113—The most losses by a Pirates club (1890), when it played only 136 games.

FIELD MANAGERS

Every American male swears he can do three things better than
the professionals:
1. Run a hotel
2. Grill a steak
3. Manage a Major League Baseball team

Perhaps that's why Danny Murtaugh—a four-time Buccos
skipper—once said, "Why certainly I'd like to have that fellow
who hits a home run every time at bat, who strikes out every
opposing batter when he's pitching, who throws strikes to any
base or the plate when he's playing outfield, and who's always
thinking about two innings ahead just what he'll do to baffle the
other team. Any manager would want a guy like that playing for
him. The only trouble is to get him to put down his cup of beer
and come down out of the stands and do those things."

The Pittsburgh Pirates, throughout their history, have introduced their share of both good and not-so-good managers. Fans
have not always agreed about who belongs in which category.

No fewer than 10 managers were responsible for guiding the
Pittsburgh franchise in the National League over its first 13 years:

Name	Years Managed	Record
Horace Phillips	1887–1889	149–180
Fred Dunlap	1889	7–10
Ned Hanlon	1889, 1891	57–65
Guy Hecker	1890	23–113
Bill McGunnigle	1891	24–33
Tom Burns	1892	27–32
Al Buckenberger	1892–1894	187–144
Connie Mack	1894–1896	149–134
Patsy Donovan	1897–1899	129–129
Bill Watkins	1898–1899	79–91

By the time Pittsburgh acquired players such as Honus Wagner
from the defunct Louisville Colonels prior to the 1900 season, the
role of the Pirates manager became much more important. Not

only had the game become more sophisticated, but also certain players were now household names. The term *superstar* may not as yet have been used by reporters; however, the concept was alive and well. A manager now had to know about the fine points of baseball, as well as be a counselor, a father figure, and a psychologist, just to keep the players content and playing their best.

Filling the shoes of a skipper in the show is not easy. If a team wins, players get the credit; if it loses, the manager is the first to be criticized. It's grossly unjust, but it comes with the territory. The age-old truth is, "There are but two kinds of managers—those who have been fired and those who will be fired."

Here are thumbnail sketches of the men who have accepted the challenge of serving as manager of the Pittsburgh Pirates during the modern era.

Fred Clarke

Years Managed: 1900–1915
Record: 1,422–969
League Titles: 1901, 1902, 1903, 1909
World Championships: 1909
Of Interest: Fred Clarke may have been ahead of his time in terms of initiating strategies for the modern manager. He had, for instance, a unique, yet effective, way of bringing up pitchers. Instead of starting a raw rookie against seasoned veterans, he kept him in the bullpen to work on technique. When the time was right, he put him into a game for an inning or so to allow the youngster to gain the confidence necessary to win in the big leagues.

Jimmy "Nixey" Callahan

Years Managed: 1916–1917
Record: 85–129
League Titles: 0
World Championships: 0
Of Interest: Following their poor record in Jimmy Callahan's first season as manager in 1916, the Pirates were even worse the next year. Eventually, the situation became too much for this strict

disciplinarian to bear, and he mysteriously disappeared from the team for 10 days on an alcoholic bender. As a result, he was summarily dismissed by owner Barney Dreyfuss.

Honus Wagner
Years Managed: 1917
Record: 1–4
League Titles: 0
World Championships: 0
Of Interest: The Flying Dutchman may have become a superb manager, but he let it be known that he never wanted to be strapped with this responsibility. Perhaps his record after only five days at the helm helped in his making that decision.

Hugo Bezdek
Years Managed: 1917–1919
Record: 166–187
League Titles: 0
World Championships: 0
Of Interest: This former All-American fullback for the University of Chicago and football coach at several universities was able to ride out the remainder of the 1917 season. He then instilled a rigorous conditioning program for Pirates players that helped them compile two seasons of better than .500 ball. Football, however, was Bezdek's first love, and he left the Pirates after 1919 to accept a position as head football coach and athletics director at Penn State University.

George Gibson
Years Managed: 1920–1922, 1932–1934
Record: 401–330
League Titles: 0
World Championships: 0
Of Interest: Nicknamed Moon because of his round face, George Gibson, a former catcher with the Pirates (1905–1916), was popular among the players. His easy-going manner, however, resulted in a lack of discipline that seemed to prevent the Pirates

from playing up to their potential. He was eventually replaced near the end of the 1922 season, but he was called on by Dreyfuss 10 years later in a futile attempt to rejuvenate the club.

Bill McKechnie
Years Managed: 1922–1926
Record: 409–293
League Titles: 1925
World Championships: 1925
Of Interest: This native of Wilkinsburg, Pennsylvania, was the handpicked choice of Dreyfuss to replace George Gibson. Nicknamed the Deacon because he served as an elder at his church in Wilkinsburg, Bill McKechnie was unable to curtail the wild nightlife of some of his star players, including Rabbit Maranville. Although he was able to win the 1925 World Series

WHO'S IN CHARGE AROUND HERE?

During his second year as manager of the Pittsburgh Pirates, Fred Clarke was irritated at the Bucs' ragged play, which resulted in a string of losses. Following one especially dismal defeat, the fiery Clarke summoned the team into the locker room for a private meeting.

Clarke wasn't alone in his anger. Owner Barney Dreyfuss, with a set jaw and clenched fists, followed Clarke into the clubhouse and was prepared to add to the tongue-lashing.

When he saw the owner standing behind him, Clarke abruptly turned and looked him squarely in the eye. "Get out and stay out!" he shouted to his boss.

Dreyfuss was aghast. "You mean I can't come into my own clubhouse?" he asked.

"Exactly!" Clarke said. "Anytime you want to find fault with the team, you talk to me in private. I'll take the blame. As far as these players, if there is criticism, they'll hear plenty from me and me alone."

Dreyfuss knew Clarke was right and seldom set foot again in the locker room immediately before or after a game.

BY THE NUMBERS

.309—Highest team batting average for the Bucs (1928)

against Washington, he left the next year due in part to disagreements with former manager Fred Clarke, who had been hired as Major League Baseball's first "bench coach."

Donie Bush
Years Managed: 1927–1929
Record: 246–178
League Titles: 1927
World Championships: 0
Of Interest: Owner Barney Dreyfuss wanted a no-nonsense manager to corral his players, whom he felt had taken advantage of the subdued McKechnie. He chose the 16-year veteran shortstop Donie Bush. At first it appeared that Dreyfuss had made the right choice, as the Pirates clawed their way to the National League pennant. However, the stubborn Bush refused to work out differences with his star player, Kiki Cuyler, and benched him for the remainder of the season and the World Series, which the Bucs dropped to the Yankees in four games.

Jewel Ens
Years Managed: 1929–1931
Record: 176–167
League Titles: 0
World Championships: 0
Of Interest: Jewel Ens was a classic example of someone who was in the wrong place at the wrong time. Being popular with the players and guiding the Pirates to a winning season in 1930, despite having the league's second-worst pitching staff, did not result in a long-term contract. As a result, the timid, low-key Ens was let go following the 1931 season, the club's first losing campaign since 1917.

Pie Traynor

Years Managed: 1934–1939
Record: 457–406
League Titles: 0
World Championships: 0
Of Interest: Former Pirates first baseman (1930–1939) Gus Suhr once said of Pie Traynor, "He's a good manager, but maybe a little too nice for the job." That would be a fair appraisal. Guiding teams to four winning seasons in the six he managed, Traynor was held in high esteem by both players and fans. Without an ace pitcher on the roster, Traynor did as much as anyone could possibly have done to keep the Pirates in contention. After he realized he would not be rehired following the '39 season, Traynor resigned as manager, to the dismay of Pirates fans, but remained with the club as a scout and a coach until his death in 1972.

A rare photograph shows Pirates great Pie Traynor, when he was manager of the club, with a young Ford Frick, then a newspaper reporter who would become president of the National League and, later, commissioner of Major League Baseball. (Photo courtesy of the National Baseball Hall of Fame)

Frankie Frisch
Years Managed: 1940–1946
Record: 539–528
League Titles: 0
World Championships: 0
Of Interest: One of baseball's few college graduates at that time, the Fordham Flash got off to a good start with winning seasons during his first two years at the helm. However, because of his abrasive manner cultivated while managing the infamous Gas House Gang of the St. Louis Cardinals, Frisch clashed with some of his star players as well as with umpires. Coupled with the World War II draft depleting the club of other rising stars, Frisch did not enjoy the success he had with the Redbirds. When the Dreyfuss family sold the Pirates to John Galbreath's group, the team was floundering in seventh place, and Frisch was discharged three games prior to the 1946 season's conclusion.

Virgil "Spud" Davis
Years Managed: 1946
Record: 1–2
League Titles: 0
World Championships: 0
Of Interest: This former catcher had a .308 lifetime average and was the "mop-up man" following Frankie Frisch's dismissal. He remained with the Pirates as a coach.

Billy Herman
Years Managed: 1947
Record: 61–92
League Titles: 0
World Championships: 0
Of Interest: Billy Herman came to Pittsburgh from the Boston Braves with the challenge to be a player/manager who would turn the team around. In exchange, the Bucs gave up third baseman Bob Elliott. The result: Elliott would go on to win the MVP award that season, while Herman came up with a sore arm and was able to play in only 15 games. As a result of his team's tying for last

place in the National League, Pirates president Frank McKinney released Herman on the evening before the last game of the season.

Bill Burwell
Years Managed: 1947
Record: 1–0
League Titles: 0
World Championships: 0
Of Interest: Replacing Billy Herman as manager for the final game of the 1947 season, Bill Burwell, a coach with the club, is one of the few people who can boast of a perfect record as a Major League Baseball manager.

Billy Meyer
Years Managed: 1948–1952
Record: 317–452
League Titles: 0
World Championships: 0
Of Interest: During Billy Meyer's first year as manager, it looked as though the Bucs might take it all. Although Pittsburgh had to be satisfied with a fourth-place finish, for which Meyer was named *The Sporting News* Manager of the Year, all of Pittsburgh was excited about the team's prospects. Alas, those hopes faded as fast as an early-morning fog over the Allegheny River, despite the fact that the team featured the league's home-run champion, Ralph Kiner, throughout Meyer's tenure. After slogging through the next four years, ending with the horrible '52 campaign and its 112 losses, Meyer was gone. Perhaps as a way of saying "We're sorry for all we put you through," the Bucs retired his No. 1 in 1954.

Fred Haney
Years Managed: 1953–1955
Record: 163–299
League Titles: 0
World Championships: 0
Of Interest: Prior to the 1953 season, new manager Fred Haney promised only that his team would not lose 112 games. He

YOU SAID WHAT?

Pirates manager Fred Clarke often embarrassed Barney Dreyfuss with his boisterous on-field outbursts at umpires that were usually peppered with obscenities. One arbiter who was the target of a particularly salty tirade from Clarke was James "Bug" Holliday.

The arbiter was having a rough time behind home plate one afternoon, which could explain why he spent only one year in the majors. Following an obviously missed called strike, the Pirates player/manager ran in from his position in left field and levied a blistering verbal attack on the umpire that would have caused even a steel mill worker to blush.

Holliday had taken enough and gave Clarke the thumb.

The umpire confessed later that he had not realized the full impact of Clarke's attack. "I knew what he called me must have been some bad names," he said, "but only after I went to my hotel room and looked up those words in a dictionary did I know just how bad they really were."

succeeded by winning eight more than his predecessor did. A quiet man by nature, Haney sealed his fate when he openly criticized Pirates general manager Branch Rickey, who had ordered him to concentrate on playing some young ballplayers instead of winning ballgames.

Bobby Bragan
Years Managed: 1956–1957
Record: 102–155
League Titles: 0
World Championships: 0
Of Interest: A disciple of Branch Rickey, Bobby Bragan had earned a reputation around baseball circles as a hothead. His flamboyant, verbal attacks on umpires included once appearing from the dugout, following his fourth ejection in 1957, with a cup of orange juice and suggesting that he and the home-plate umpire "talk it over."

Danny Murtaugh

Years Managed: 1957–1964, 1967, 1970–1971, 1973–1976
Record: 1,115–950
Division Titles: 1960, 1971, 1974, 1975
League Titles: 1960, 1971
World Championships: 1960, 1971
Of Interest: One of the most fortunate moves ever made by the Pirates was acquiring Danny Murtaugh from the Boston Braves' organization in 1948 as a "utility" second baseman. Murtaugh ended the year as the starting second sacker, batting .290 and leading the league in putouts, assists, and double plays. That was his introduction into the Pirates family. When he was named manager,

Prior to the 1960 World Series, Pirates manager Danny Murtaugh meets with former manager Bill McKechnie.

193

this popular Irishman from Chester, Pennsylvania, with a delicious sense of humor, endured some challenging seasons with players who showed limited ability. He led the Bucs to two World Series championships. The Pirates retired his No. 40 in 1977.

Harry Walker

Years Managed: 1965–1967
Record: 224–84
League Titles: 0
World Championships: 0
Of Interest: Harry "the Hat" Walker was an evangelist of sound hitting techniques. His prize students included Roberto Clemente and Matty Alou—both of whom won batting titles. The man who was awarded a Bronze Star and a Purple Heart for bravery in World War II was also a master motivator who pushed the Bucs into pennant contention during his first two years as manager. When his magic touch suddenly disappeared in '67, he was released by general manager Joe L. Brown.

Larry Shepard

Years Managed: 1968–1969
Record: 164–155
League Titles: 0
World Championships: 0
Of Interest: Larry Shepard was a class act who knew baseball. Unfortunately, he was unable to communicate effectively with his players. Sometimes his mental lapses during a game resulted in needless losses. When he instituted a five-man rotation for the pitching staff with the idea of keeping his hurlers fresh, his mound staff rebelled. Pressure mounted until, in 1969, he missed nine games after collapsing due to a circulatory problem. Although the club was certain to end the season with a winning record, general manager Joe L. Brown fired him with five games remaining. The reason Brown gave was that Shepard was "just not the right man for the post."

Alex Grammas
Years Managed: 1969
Record: 4–1
League Titles: 0
World Championships: 0
Of Interest: Following 10 years as a player in the major leagues, Alex "the Golden Greek" Grammas got his first chance to manage when he took over for the departed Larry Shepard for the final five games of the '69 season. The Golden Greek went on to coach in Cincinnati under his mentor, future Hall of Famer Sparky Anderson, and later managed the Milwaukee Brewers before rejoining Anderson in Detroit.

Bill Virdon
Years Managed: 1972–1973
Record: 163–128
Division Title: 1972
League Titles: 0
World Championships: 0
Of Interest: To be asked to follow a manager as popular as Danny Murtaugh and take the reins of a club that had won the World Series the year before, and to do this in Major League Baseball's first strike-shortened season, is more than unfair. Bill Virdon, however, was up to the task. He guided the Pirates to a 96–59 record—a better percentage than the year before—to win the National League East. Hopes for a repeat as world champions went up in smoke with a heartbreaking loss to the Cincinnati Reds in the deciding game of the NLCS. The untimely death of Roberto Clemente and a mysterious disappearance of control by his ace pitcher, Steve Blass, contributed to diminishing returns from the team in 1973. After quietly turning over the keys to the manager's office once again to Murtaugh, Virdon became a manager for the New York Yankees, Houston Astros, and Montreal Expos. Today, he serves the Pirates as a coach at spring training.

Chuck Tanner

Years Managed: 1977–1985
Record: 711–685
Division Titles: 1979
League Titles: 1979
World Championships: 1979
Of Interest: The theme song for the 1979 world champion Pirates was "We Are Family." Mostly responsible for this attitude was manager Chuck Tanner. Molding a team of strong personalities could be a challenge to the most sophisticated psychologist. Tanner, a New Castle, Pennsylvania, native, was able to pull the right strings and orchestrate a team of winners that proudly adopted the tag "Chuck's Bucs." He also led teams to pennant races in 1982 and 1983. The bottom dropped out quickly after that, ending with a horrible season in 1985, highlighted by a drug scandal in the Pirates clubhouse that shook all of baseball.

Jim Leyland

Years Managed: 1986–1996
Record: 851–863
Division Titles: 1990, 1991, 1992
League Titles: 0
World Championships: 0
Of Interest: To Jim Leyland, baseball was a game, and everyone on the staff should have fun while in uniform. Former players still heap praise on him as being one of the finest managers in the game and one for whom it was easy to play. In 1990, he won his first Manager of the Year award (he also won in 1992 and 2006) when he guided the team to the National League Eastern Division title, only to lose to Cincinnati in the NLCS, four games to two. The Pirates won the National League East again in 1991, losing the NLCS to Atlanta in seven games. In 1992, history repeated itself, as former Pirate Sid Bream scored the winning run in the last of the ninth to defeat Leyland's Bucs for the National League pennant. Disappointments such as these, plus the realization that Kevin McClatchy and the new owners of the club were unable to

spend big money in order to acquire solid players, convinced Leyland to tender his resignation.

Gene Lamont

Years Managed: 1997–2000
Record: 295–352
League Titles: 0
World Championships: 0
Of Interest: Following the last game at Three Rivers Stadium on October 1, 2000, players from the present and past were introduced to the sellout crowd. The loudest ovation that night was saved for Lamont, who had just completed his last game as Bucs manager. By this gesture, the astute Pittsburgh fans showed the departing manager that they realized he was not at fault for the faltering teams of the past four years. They also showed how much they respected the classy way in which the skipper had conducted himself through four years of frustration.

Lloyd McClendon

Years Managed: 2001–2005
Record: 336–446
League Titles: 0
World Championships: 0
Of Interest: Lloyd McClendon will probably be remembered best not as Pittsburgh's first African American manager, but as one who gave the most aggressive demonstration of his anger at what he perceived to be bad calls by umpires. On June 26, 2001, he felt he and his team were getting the short end of the stick from umpiring decisions. Following his ejection from the game, McClendon grabbed the first-base bag, yanked it from the ground,

BY THE NUMBERS

.231—The lowest team batting average for the team, posted by the 1952 Pirates.

and abruptly left the field of play. His intensity, however, was not enough to motivate the Bucs to winning seasons in any of his five years at the helm.

Pete Mackanin

Years Managed: 2005
Record: 12–14
League Titles: 0
World Championships: 0
Of Interest: As interim manager for the Pirates' final 26 games following the dismissal of McClendon, Mackanin was a perfect person to fill that role. He was the bench coach for his predecessor, thus he knew his players and could help pave the way for the new full-time skipper.

Jim Tracy

Years Managed: 2006–2007
Record: 135–189
League Titles: 0
World Championships: 0
Of Interest: Jim Tracy, a former basketball All-American at Ohio's Marietta College, has an extensive background in developing team play. In his first year with the Bucs, Tracy initially found it difficult to relate to the media, sometimes showing impatience with reporters' questions. As the season and the team matured, both he and the media finally saw positive results of his leadership as the team played better than .500 ball during the last half of the 2006 season. After leading the team to its 15th consecutive losing season, the mild-mannered Tracy was dismissed at the end of the 2007 season. He was replaced by John Russell.

SOCIAL PROGRESS

Prior to 1947, the only colors (other than white) on a baseball diamond were the green grass and brown dirt of the infield. With the signing of Jack Roosevelt Robinson (he never liked the name "Jackie") by the Brooklyn Dodgers, this all changed. Slowly, other clubs followed suit.

Pittsburgh was the 10th club in Major League Baseball to sign a minority player (Curtis Roberts), seven years after Robinson broke the unwritten barrier to African Americans.

The last team to break the color barrier was the Boston Red Sox in July 1959.

Over the past few years, the number of African Americans in the big leagues has dwindled in percentage due to several factors, including the sharp rise in talent of players from Latin America and the Far East, primarily Japan.

This final chapter reveals some behind-the-scenes looks at the early days of integration by the Pittsburgh Pirates.

CHANGING THE COLOR OF THE GAME

The civil rights movement in America began not in 1965 with an organized march across the Edmund Pettus Bridge in Selma, Alabama, but nearly two decades earlier at first base in a National League baseball park in Brooklyn, New York.

Prior to Opening Day 1947, Major League Baseball was, for all practical purposes, an all-white, good ol' boys' club. With the rare exception of the names of a few Native Americans and some imported Cubans who had appeared earlier on rosters of both National League and American League teams, a so-called unwritten rule imposed by baseball commissioner Kenesaw Mountain Landis permitted no big-league team to sign a "person of color."

The ban should not imply to 21st-century readers that African Americans of that era lacked major league talent. In fact, the opposite was true. Stars such as Leroy "Satchel" Paige, Josh Gibson, Buck Leonard, and James "Cool Papa" Bell played in the Negro Leagues for teams such as the Chattanooga Black Lookouts, the Newark Eagles, the Birmingham Black Barons, plus two representatives of Allegheny County, Pennsylvania—the Homestead Grays and the Pittsburgh Crawfords.

Each of those athletes, and many others, embodied enough talent to make any team in the majors. However, before that would be possible, two things had to occur: (1) The nation would have to change its views about race, and (2) Baseball had to get a new commissioner.

Before the first condition had time to materialize, Landis died in 1944. Owners then selected former Kentucky governor Albert B. "Happy" Chandler to replace Landis.

Baseball gurus assumed that the new commissioner, who was raised in the segregated South, would naturally continue the ban on African American players. They, and others, were wrong. Chandler had absolutely no problem with allowing people of all colors to attend tryout camps and openly compete for positions on major league rosters.

That opened the door for influential people, such as general manager Branch Rickey of the Brooklyn Dodgers, to initiate changes. Rickey, who would join the front office of the Pirates a few years later, saw the potential of an increase in both wins and home attendance once he brought in some African American players. The first person he signed was 27-year-old Jack Roosevelt "Jackie" Robinson, a product of Cairo, Georgia.

Robinson was selected by Rickey partly because he was an outstanding athlete at UCLA, and also because he possessed what Rickey believed was the sort of attitude that would allow him to endure harsh criticisms directed at an African American who, in their opinion, "dared" to infiltrate a heretofore "Caucasians-only" branch of society.

Those of us who live in modern times may have a bit of difficulty understanding just how harsh life had been in this era for those who were not born a "WASP" (White Anglo-Saxon Protestant). Black soldiers served in segregated units throughout World War II. Congress could not even get a vote on the floor of the United States Senate for legislation to outlaw lynching. Public waiting rooms for trains and buses were labeled "White" and "Colored." And heaven help the young black teenage boy who dared to whistle at an attractive white girl.

Branch Rickey signed Robinson to a contract three years before President Truman's executive order to integrate the army.

What made the signing of Jackie Robinson so special was that it involved a team sport that just happened to be our national pastime. Baseball's prohibition against black players was the first segregation barrier to fall. Many players and fans, however, were slow to endorse the change.

Robinson put Rickey's faith in him to a test when he was invited to the 1946 spring-training site for the Dodgers' top minor-league franchise, the Montreal Royals. While playing in Daytona Beach, Florida, Robinson and his team were prohibited from participating in games in nearby Jacksonville. In addition to catcalls cascading from the stands, he was forced to endure the taunting by one of the opposing players, who let a black cat out of the dugout to walk in front of Robinson, who was kneeling in the on-deck circle.

Robinson got the nod to wear the uniform of the parent club in 1947. It was shortly thereafter he learned that the demons of racial prejudice came not just from the camps of the enemies but also from within his own clubhouse. Key players for the Dodgers organization, such as Alabama-born outfielder Fred "Dixie" Walker, openly spoke against allowing a Negro to infiltrate their club. Walker was traded to Pittsburgh the next season.

The negative reaction to an African American player appearing in big-league baseball spilled over into the locker room of the Pittsburgh Pirates in 1947 when the players called for a vote on whether they should play on the same field with Brooklyn's Robinson. However, no ballot was ever cast. Convincing them to forget the vote was a 6'4", 210-pound first baseman who urged them, instead, to go out onto the field and play the game as best they could.

The name of this persuasive giant of a man was Henry Benjamin Greenberg, a fearsome slugger who was signed by the Pirates a few months earlier.

Greenberg, the American League's home-run king the previous year, had set Hall of Fame numbers when he challenged Babe Ruth's record by slamming 58 homers as a Detroit Tiger in 1938. Although he had missed four of his prime years to military service during World War II, Greenberg had earned the respect of teammates and opposing players alike by hitting more than 300 home runs in just nine full seasons.

Greenberg knew what it meant to be a minority (even before that term was used) baseball player in America. As a practicing Jew, he made headlines in 1934 when he refused to play in a late September game because it fell on the highest of Jewish holidays—Yom Kippur, the Day of Atonement.

"During my first full year in the big leagues [1933]," recalled Greenberg, "the remarks from the stands and the opposing bench about my Jewish faith made life for me a living hell. But I was determined not to let that interfere with my concentration on the game. I owed my people that much."

Greenberg's ability to persuade his fellow Pirates to accept the new reality of the times was a turning point in race relations for America's pastime. Some who were present in the dugout, such as the late hurler Truett Banks "Rip" Sewell, were convinced that had the Pirates boycotted the games, other clubs certainly would have followed.

On Tuesday, May 15, of that year, Robinson's team, the Dodgers, came to Forbes Field to open a three-game series against the Bucs. By this time, the slings and arrows thrown at him by fans and opposing players were testing the patience of the young man. Robinson was fielding ground balls during the pregame warm-up when Hammerin' Hank Greenberg walked from the dugout behind first base and approached Robinson. According to his son, Steve, Greenberg called Robinson to his side and spent a considerable amount of time encouraging him to curtail any urge to fight back. He cited his own experience as proof that excellent play on the field eventually can overcome all the prejudicial remarks by those who were unwilling to accept him.

Robinson later testified that this was a pivotal moment for him and was instrumental in his ability to deal with the avalanche of racial prejudice he faced for the remainder of his 10 years in Major League Baseball.

Before he died at his home in Plant City, Florida, in 1989, Rip Sewell, by then a double amputee resulting from diabetes, often spoke to reporters about that 1947 vote taken in the Pirates clubhouse. "It's difficult to imagine," he said, "what might have happened to baseball that year had we voted against playing on the same baseball diamond as Jackie Robinson."

Greenberg finished his only season at Pittsburgh that year by hitting 25 out of the park and batting, for him at least, a modest .249. Perhaps his biggest legacy as a Pirate was his schooling of a young Ralph Kiner, whom he tutored during hours of extra batting practice on the importance of standing closer to the plate to pull more pitches over the left-field fences. Greenberg proved to be an excellent coach, as Kiner hit 51 home runs to lead the league that year.

MAJOR LEAGUE BASEBALL'S FIRST ALL-MINORITY LINEUP

September 1, 1971, will probably not go down in the annals of baseball as a hallmark date, although it should.

Some 11,278 fans assembled at Three Rivers Stadium to see a significant night game between the Pittsburgh Pirates and the Philadelphia Phillies. Someone might argue that all games that year for Pittsburgh were significant, since the Pirates were leading the Eastern Division of the National League by just a few games over St. Louis. Also, this was the year in which the national media caught up with something that Pirates fans had known for years—Roberto Clemente was the finest right fielder in the game.

Clemente had everything you could ask for in a ballplayer. He possessed the speed of Willie Mays, the arm of Carl Furillo, and the sure hands of Joe DiMaggio.

On that first night in September the fans were surprised in a way that came without any fanfare. Everything seemed normal when manager Danny Murtaugh presented the starting lineup to home-plate umpire Stan Landes a few minutes prior to the game. It wasn't until the home team Pirates took to the field that the more astute fan noticed something unusual. Taking their positions for the Bucs were:

First Base—Al Oliver
Second Base—Rennie Stennett
Shortstop—Jackie Hernandez
Third Base—Dave Cash
Left Field—Willie Stargell
Center Field—Gene Clines
Right Field—Roberto Clemente
Catcher—Manny Sanguillen
Pitcher—Dock Ellis

What was so strange about this group of Pirates?

It wasn't that the Pirates won the game that evening, 10–7. Or that Sanguillen had smacked a home run. Or even that Clines and Cash each stole a base. Of much greater significance was the fact that this was the first time in the history of Major League Baseball that any team had filled its starting lineup with all minority players.

Murtaugh had not planned this. To the contrary, he was totally oblivious to the milestone that resulted when he penned the names of the starting nine on the scorecard, until he met with reporters who were standing outside his clubhouse office following the game.

Some of the reporters had whispered among themselves that this might have been some sort of publicity stunt. One of his coaches clued in the jovial Pirates manager about these rumors. Murtaugh immediately rose from his desk and walked out among the reporters. His first mission was to put those thoughts to rest when he spoke before anyone had an opportunity to raise a question: "I put the best nine athletes out there. The best nine I put out there tonight happened to be black. No big deal. Next question."

THE BUCS' FIRST MINORITY PLAYER

When Curtis Benjamin Roberts stepped to the plate in Forbes Field on Opening Day 1954, Pittsburgh fans saw something they had never before seen—an African American wearing a Pirates uniform. The moment Roberts lined a triple to left-center field, color made no difference. The partisan crowd cheered in appreciation.

The Bucs introduced their new second baseman with not as much anxiety as the Dodgers had seven years earlier when Jackie Robinson integrated Major League Baseball. Generally speaking, the club accepted him. Nellie King, one of his teammates, said, "We didn't think of him as a black guy. He was just a player. He could be a pain in the ass at times and a real nice kid at times, just like anyone else."

The Pirates did insist, however, that Roberts room alone on road trips, since big-league baseball still had an unwritten policy of not integrating roommates. Also, some hotels in visiting towns refused to house African Americans.

Roberts, an excellent fielder, hit only .223 in 171 games over the three years (1954–1956) he played for the Pirates. His chances for any genuine future with the club were curtailed with the arrival of a rookie named Bill Mazeroski.

SOURCES

Adomites, Paul, and Saul Wisnia, *Best of Baseball* (Lincolnwood, IL: Publications International, Ltd., 1997).

Alexander, Charles, *Our Game* (New York: MJF Books, 1991).

Aylesworth, Thomas, and Benton Minks, *The Encyclopedia of Baseball Managers* (New York: Crescent Books, 1990).

Finoli, David, and Bill Ranier, *The Pittsburgh Pirates Encyclopedia* (Champaign, IL: Sports Publishing, LLC, 2003).

Hageman, William, *Honus* (Champaign, IL: Sagamore Publishing, 1996).

Honig, Donald, *When the Grass Was Real* (Lincoln: University of Nebraska Press, 1975).

James, Bill, *The Bill James Guide to Baseball Managers* (New York: Schribner, 1949).

Kiner, Ralph, *Baseball Forever* (Chicago: Triumph Press, 2004).

Kiner, Ralph, *Kiner's Korner* (New York: Arbor House, 1987).

Leventhal, Josh, *Take Me Out to the Ballpark* (New York: Black Dog & Leventhal Publishers, 2006).

Lieb, Frederick, *The Pittsburgh Pirates* (New York: G.P. Putnam's Sons, 1948).

McCollister, John C., *Tales from the Pirates Dugout* (Champaign, IL: Sports Publishing, LLC, 2003).

McCollister, John, *Tales from the 1979 Pittsburgh Pirates* (Champaign, IL: Sports Publishing, LLC, 2005).

McCollister, John, *The Bucs! The Story of the Pittsburgh Pirates* (Lenexa, KS: Addax Publishing Group, 1998).

McCollister, John, *The Best Baseball Games Ever Played* (New York: Citadel/Kensington Press, 2002).

Nemec, David, and Saul Wisnia, *100 Years of Major League Baseball* (Lincolnwood, IL: Publications International, Ltd., 2000).

Ritter, Lawrence S., *The Glory of Their Times* (New York: William Morrow, 1984).

Shribman, David, ed., *Sports Town—Sports Pages of The Post-Gazette* (Pittsburgh: *The Post-Gazette*, 2004).

Solomon, Burt, *Baseball Timeline* (New York: Avon Books, 1997).

Thorn, John, ed., *The National Pastime* (New York: Warner Books, 1987).

Thorn, John, et al., *Total Baseball* (New York: Viking, 1997).

Wolff, Rick, et al., *The Baseball Encyclopedia* (New York: Macmillan Publishing Co., 1993).

.